THE

COMING

OF

Order this book online at www.trafford.com
or email orders@trafford.com

Most Trafford titles are also available at major online book retailers.

Printed in Victoria, BC, Canada.

ISBN: 978-1-4269-3358-5 (sc)

ISBN: 978-1-4269-3359-2 (hc)

Library of Congress Control Number: 2010907740

Our mission is to efficiently provide the world's finest, most comprehensive book publishing service, enabling every author to experience success. To find out how to publish your book, your way, and have it available worldwide, visit us online at www.trafford.com

Trafford rev. 6/3/2010

Trafford
PUBLISHING® www.trafford.com

North America & international
toll-free: 1 888 232 4444 (USA & Canada)
phone: 250 383 6864 ♦ fax: 812 355 4082

Contents

1.	The ONE	1
2.	Human Adventure	4
3.	Travel & Bodies	7
4.	Earth	10
5.	Earth Souls	14
6.	Visitation of G.O.D	17
7.	The Emissary	19
8.	Time For a Correction	24
9.	The Life of James	29
10.	The Mission Begins	32
11.	Learning	35
12.	Home	40
13.	Back to the Task	43
14.	Journeying	47
15.	Catastrophe	51
16.	Exploring	54
17.	A Shamanic Adventure	61
18.	Lessons in Reality	70
19.	Helena	75
20.	A New Beginning	80

21.	N D Es	83
22.	The Family	86
23.	The Community	89
24.	Venerable	95
25.	Changeover	101
26.	Cave of Bones	106
27.	Back to Work	110
28.	The Final Days	118

The ONE

In the beginning there was confusion; the Universe was unorganized, which resulted in many collisions between the different sized blobs of material that were floating in space as a result of the many exploding bodies. At some point in time Universal Intelligence began to assemble the entire masses into a definable pattern, Solar systems came into existence, and there was a distinct pattern to all the mass that existed.

As the Universal Intelligence grew, learned and created an ever more magnificent system of Planets, and Solar Systems It soon became known as simply The ONE. The ONE was aware that It had created many magnificent bodies in the Universe, these bodies, which would soon become known as Planets contained many wonders of Creation, but The ONE had no way of gauging the magnificence of Its works.

The ONE rested, and began to ponder what had been created. The ONE realized It had to create another entity that would be able to experience all of Creation, and then bring the memory of that experience back to The ONE so that It too would know the wonder of all that It had created. Thus The ONE divided into infinitesimal smaller entities, which would be known as Spirits, retained the Essence of The ONE, retained all the powers of The ONE, and were given the ability to traverse Creation experiencing all that was. After the Spirits had

1

experienced all there was they would return to The ONE, rejoin The ONE, and share all of the experiences so that The ONE would know the magnificence of Creation.

The Spirits set out to experience the Universe that had been created, it was soon apparent that they could see the wonders of the Universe, but they had no sense of what it consisted of. How it smelled, What did it taste like, How did it feel, and Where could the Spirits find a method of truly experiencing all that was.

As the Spirits moved around the Universe they began to see creatures that were evolving from the primordial elements found on some of the planets. There were huge lumbering beasts, plants of all kinds, fish of all sorts swimming in the waters of the planets, but all of these entities seemed to be restricted in their movements, confined to their own environment with no opportunity of moving out into the Universe.

Then in one instance the Spirits discovered a huge creature on one of the Planets in the center of the Universe, the Spirits named the planet Sirius B. This creature walked upright on sturdy legs, moved around at will, had upper limbs that were attached to the upper body, with smaller limbs at the very end of these arms. The head of this creature was round, and had orifices that allowed the creature to see, hear, and smell its environment.

The Spirits decided that they should occupy one of these creatures to see if it would be possible to physically experience the environment, using the huge man's senses. To the Spirits ultimate enjoyment it was found that YES they could smell, hear, and see the environment of this creature. They called this creature "Human", and began to occupy the species in mass, so that soon most all of the Humans had a Spirit occupying them.

It soon became apparent that the Spirits, due to them occupying older Humans, and not the newly created ones, were not enjoying some of the Human experience. They decided that it would be better to enter the Humans at the moment the Humans entered the environment, so it was that from that point on when ever a Human was born into the environment, a Spirit entered the body, and experienced all that happened to the body as it grew into adulthood.

The Human experience was confined to a Planet orbiting a Star in the center of the Universe, because try as they might the Spirits could find no equivalent Creatures elsewhere in the Universe. It was decided that the intelligence quotient of the Humans would be developed to the point they would be able to travel about the Universe, and physically experience the magnificence of it.

Human Adventure

The Spirits began to enhance the Human intelligence, but still allowed the Humans to have the freedom of choosing which path they would follow in the development of their lives. The only Spiritual content that was imparted into the Human psyche was the knowledge that all were part of The ONE, and each had an infinitesimal part of The ONE at its very center.

There were specific divisions within the Human colony, each with a distinctive color to set it apart from the others, there were White, Black, Red, Brown, and Yellow colored Humans. Each of these colors became known as Races, and soon gathered in separate areas of the Planet. Some of the Races began to develop intelligence very quickly, which led to jealousy on the part of the Races that were not keeping pace developing their intelligence. This jealousy led to the undeveloped Races attacking the developed Race, this soon became known on the Planet as "War".

Over time the capabilities of the Races to wage War with one another led to more and more destructive methods of annihilating the other side, until it appeared as though all Humans would be gone from the Planet. At this point the Spirits decided to step in and halt the practice of War. They did this by controlling the elements so that neither side could attack the other. When the Races found they could no longer wage War with each other they decided to halt all aggressive acts towards one another.

The Humans developed a code of conduct to follow, which became the law of those whose body was occupied by a Spirit. The Law was given to all Humans with the intent that all should follow the Law, and live in peace with their fellow Humans. The Law had 7 basic tenants:

1. 'Remember the Sabbath day, to keep it holy.'
2. 'Honor your father and your mother.'
3. 'Do not kill another human.'
4. 'Do not engage in Sexual Relations while unmarried'
5. 'Do not steal.'
6. 'Do not bear false witness against your neighbor.'
7. 'You shall not covet your neighbor's house; you shall not covet your neighbor's wife, nor his male servant, nor his female servant, nor anything else that is your neighbor's

As soon as Humans began to follow these simple Laws civilization on the Planet began to rapidly develop in all Races. Cooperation amongst the Races led to the formation of a group to govern the Planet, and provide guidance to all that existed there, this group became known as "Council of the Collective" because it represented every Race equally so the all Humans on the Planet were also represented in an equal manner.

At the first meeting of The Council it was decided there was a need for a Supreme leader to represent all Humans and speak on their behalf. There was a wise one who assigned tasks, duties, and domain to others within his realm. This one was known as "Giver Of Domain". The Council called upon Giver Of Domain to come and direct the activities of the Collective, they also shortened the wise one's title to "G.O.D". So it was that G.O.D became the Supreme Leader of the Collective.

There were many inhabitants of the Planet that disagreed with the formation of the Council of the Collective, and set off to form their own organizations. A leader that controlled the existence of all Humans within the organization dominated many of these organizations. These leaders became known as Dictators. Most of these Dictators did not follow the tenets of the Law, and made up their own Laws to control the Humans.

This did not please the members of the Council, and G.O.D, but it was decided that individual free will would be left to those who chose to follow the Dictators. The exodus weakened the Zones of the Collective, because the remaining Humans did not have a sufficient supply of all the necessary elements to assure their survival.

The Council decided to explore the Universe to find a secure supply of elements required to sustain constant growth in population of the Collective.

Travel & Bodies

In order for this exploration to proceed a method of travel outside the sphere of the Planet had to be devised. Scientists of the Collective had found different stones that attracted, or repelled one another depending on their proximity to one another. Also when formed into a bar the stones maintained the properties, with each end of the stone having different properties. This energy became known as magnetism; "North" and "South" poles designated each end of the bar. If a North Pole was pointed at a South Pole they immediately came together. If 2 North poles were pointed at each other they immediately repelled each other. It was also found that the power of the Magnets could be greatly enhanced if they were moved through other magnets sphere of influence.

One day a scientist dropped a small magnet, and discovered that it aligned itself in a straight line pointing to the North and South of the Planet. This discovery led to the identification of the Planet as a huge bar magnet. Indeed if the small magnets position was altered it always returned to its North South configuration. The Scientists experimented with methods of shielding the small magnet from the attraction of the Planet.

Many of the elements of the Planet were attracted to the magnets, there was one that was not, and it was easily shaped and called "Copper" by the scientists. A magnet was encased in the copper, but the power of the magnet was able to penetrate the copper and attract elements on the other side. Another element known as Iridium also appeared to be not influenced by the magnet. A layer of Iridium was placed between two sheets of Copper, and it was noted that the power of the magnet to attract other magnets outside the layers was greatly diminished. The scientists kept applying layers of Iridium, and Copper until the magnet was completely shielded, and would not have any effect on magnets or elements outside the shield.

A pot like vessel was built to house a magnet whose power could be enhanced by applying an electrical current to wires surrounding the magnet. This vessel was taken to a high hill on the planet, and its open end pointed to a nearby planet. When the power was applied to the magnet the vessel rose and headed to the nearby planet only to fall back when the power was disconnected. Thus was discovered the power unit to enable a craft to travel around the Planet.

It came to pass that an error would lead to the discovery of inter stellar travel in its simplest form. A G.O.D who was operating a large transport vessel made the mistake of applying a large magnetic force to the side of the vessel that was pointed out towards space. Instantly the vessel was drawn up and out of the atmosphere of Sirius, and propelled at great speed towards the North Pole of Pleiades. The G.O.D immediately closed the force shields of the vessel, and avoided a crash on the surface of Pleiades.

It was then discovered that the vessel could easily navigate around Pleiades using the same procedures as were used on Sirius B.

The knowledge of this discovery was shared with all scientists of the Collective, and soon led to the use of magnetic vessels in all of the Zones. A further discovery that all Planets had magnetic energy greatly expanded the zones where the vessels could travel.

The Collective initiated the training of Celestial Navigators who soon became very efficient in directing the interstellar vessels to new, and challenging destinations. The Humans of The Collective began to travel the length, and breadth of the Universe in search of basic elements.

Over the time it had taken to make the discovery to develop travel away from the planet, many other discoveries had been made, and ideas developed to make the life of Humans extendable. Early Humans were susceptible to illness due to developing viruses in their atmosphere; over time scientists developed a method of creating Human bodies that were virtually indestructible, and immune to illness. These developed bodies were without Spirit, and were inert. Early in the creation of these bodies, one of the scientists learned that it could move its Spirit from one body to the created body, and the inert body would react by assuming living qualities. The departed body wilted and became inert, but the scientist was not concerned, because its Spirit now occupied a completely indestructible body.

The development of the indestructible body caused great joy among the female inhabitants of the Planet, because it meant they no longer had to go through the rigors of having another Human being formed within their bodies, and there would no longer be lasting signs of childbirth on their bodies.

The only problem was the indestructible body did not have a Spirit at the time of its creation, and with no child birth taking place there was no way for a new Spirit to enter the Human, and grow to maturity. The Spiritual Humans were concerned about the lack of growing experience by Spirits, as it was considered vital to the development of the Spirit.

These two discoveries led to the development of interplanetary travel by the Humans, which excited the Spirits to no end because it meant they could experience more of the Universe in a physical manner.

Earth

So it was that Humans discovered an inhabited Planet in orbit around a Sun known as Siderious, this planet became known as Earth.

There were inhabitants on Earth similar in shape to the Humans of the Collective; they were similar in composition also, but existed on a primate level. Their bodies were solid, gained nourishment by consuming elements, and absorbed energy by drawing in atmosphere and then expelling it.

The Collective Humans have indestructible bodies of a similar shape to the Earth beings, but they do not consume elements to gain nourishment, and do not absorb energy by intake. The Humans of the Collective absorb energy of the Universe by direct contact.

The Council of the Collective decided there would be no contact with the primates of earth, and issued a directive to all Humans of the Collective to follow. There was to be absolutely no interaction with the Earthly primates. Any mining operations would take place without primate knowledge.

Vast supplies of Copper, and Iridium were found on Earth. The Collective decided to mine these elements, and return them to the home planet. One of the races of the Collective known as the "Annunaki" was assigned the responsibility of mining these elements. They were not used to expending physical labor, and soon sought ways of easing their burden.

They envied the primates who seemed to have nothing to do but lie around in the warm sun, and hunt various creatures to fulfill their need for nourishment.

The leader of the mining team contacted the leader of the scientists to see if there was any way of harnessing the labor of the primates to assist his team in the mining operation. The leaders of the Annunaki were called "Elohim". All of the scientists were included in the ranks of "Elohim"

An ambitious Elohim geneticist began to experiment on a certain number of the primate species. Splicing Annunaki genes into the primate enhanced the intelligence of the primate. The resultant being was called "Adamu" or "Man of Earth".

The Adamu was further developed, and soon were being used as slaves to give the Annunaki workers some rest.

Genetic manipulation was a time consuming method of creating Adamu. The Elohim decided that Adamu should be given the knowledge of procreation to accelerate their creation. The Elohim created a pleasant environment for the Adamu to dwell in while they procreated. This experiment proved to be hugely successful, and many Adamu females birthed young Adamus.

The symbol of the Genetic Corps of the Elohim worn on their uniforms was the double helix of DNA; Adamu did not recognize the symbol and referred to the Genetic Corps as "Snakes".

The creation of a new species, races within the Collective was strictly forbidden. As rumors spread about the activities of the Genetic Corps an inspection team of The Collective was dispatched to Earth to verify the existence of the Elohim's experiment, and development of a new race.

Had the Elohim left Adamu unable to reproduce on their own a new race would not have come into existence, and there would have been no violation of the Collective's Laws. Upon learning of the inspection teams pending arrival Adamu was removed from their pleasant surroundings, and hidden from the inspection team.

The inspection team did learn of the development of Adamu, and reported its finding to the Council. The Council then issued an order that all Adamu be destroyed, and sent an eradication team to Earth to carry out the destruction.

The Elohim rebelled at this order, because they had found love amongst the Adamu, and did not want the Adamu destroyed, therefore Elohim met the destruction team with force. A fierce battle ensued between the Annunaki/ Elohim forces, and the Force of the Collective that was sent to Earth to ensure the order of the Council was carried out. As the battle raged on it became clear that neither side could gain the upper hand, death and destruction rained down on the Earth.

A fraternity of females with members in every zone of The Collective; known as the Daughters Of MA or DOMA observed the fighting, and were dismayed at the consequences. The DOMA sent representatives to Earth to examine the Adamu, and try to ascertain why the Elohim were so reluctant to destroy them.

The representatives found the Adamu to be very near to the form their ancestors had taken, reported back to the DOMA that the Adamu should not be destroyed, but accepted into The Collective so long as they learned to follow the Law of the Universe, and The WAY of the Collective.

The DOMA sent their forces to intercede on behalf of the Elohim/ Annunaki; The Collective withdrew its forces. The order for the destruction of the Adamu was cancelled, and the Adamu was accepted as a Race within the Collective, with the proviso they learned to follow the Law of the Universe, and The WAY of The Collective.

During the intervening time the Adamu had been put into the general population of Earth, their offspring came into contact with members of the Annunaki race. Soon there was interbreeding between the two species, and an inter-related Human race came in to existence.

This new race when accepted into the Collective would be known as "Tarans" or Humans of Earth. The Tarans retained the ability to have a Spirit develop in their bodies after they were born of a female of the species.

Many eons had passed since Humans of the Collective were born of a Female, Human bodies are now formed of indestructible materials, and the etherical energy is induced to occupy this entity. The only problem being the formed body does not have a Spirit on its completion; therefore another source of Spirits was being sought. The ability of the Taran body to nurture a Spirit brought great joy to the Council of the Collective.

The Tarans were taught the Way of the Collective by the Annunaki/ Elohim, but only a very few Tarans chose to adhere to the Way. There was little development in the Spirits of the Taran that would lead to acceptance in to the Collective.

The Council of the Collective met and decided drastic action had to be taken to set the Tarans on the right path. An inspection team visited Earth and chose a single Taran to build a vessel with the ability to accept two of each animal species on planet Earth.

Once the task was completed the Taran was directed to gather a pair of all the animals on Earth and the Taran's family into the vessel. The Collective then sent a team of scientists to Earth, and directed that rain of immense proportions fall on Earth so as to drown every living being except those in the chosen ones vessel. When the drowning was accomplished the rain was stopped, the Earth dried, the Taran's vessel rested on the land, and all of the animals left to repopulate the Earth.

Earth Souls

A strange phenomenon occurred when all of the lives except the chosen were drowned. There was a release of Spirits as the bodies expired. These Spirits lingered in the realm of Earth, and knew not the WAY. The Spirits of the Collective learned of their presence, and sent an Emissary named "ISIS" to meet with the Spirits of Earth.

During this meeting it became apparent that the Spirits of Earth were confined to a close proximity of Earth, when they attempted to travel farther into the Universe they became totally disoriented. Needless to say the Spirits of Earth were very anxious to be freed of this impediment.

Some of the Spirits of Earth were more advanced than others, and had been accustomed to loosely following the Way. ISIS decided to form Council Of Souls to administer the rebirth of Spirits into Tarans at birth. It was also resolved that forever after the Spirits of Earth would be called "Souls".

The Souls would remain in the Realm of Earth so long as they developed, and learned the Way. Once the Souls attained the level of development equal to the Spirits of the Collective, these Souls would be given the opportunity of leaving the Realm of Earth, and joining the Spirits in the Collective.

ISIS also gave the Council of Souls the power to allow a Taran Soul to reenter the body of a Taran at the time of birth. The purpose of this reentry was to allow the Soul to improve its outlook, relationship to the Collective, and build to being able to attain the etherical levels of all other humans. The power to choose which soul could be reborn was given to the Council of Souls, which consisted of the elder souls in the Earth orbit, and those humans, which The Collective Council from time to time sent to Earth as Representatives.

The level of development was left for the Council of Souls to determine, and make recommendation to the Council of the Collective to elevate a Soul and allow it to leave the Realm of Earth.

The COS soon had many Souls wanting to be reborn on Earth so as to become more suitable to leave the Realm of Earth. Whenever it was discovered that a Taran female was with child the COS designated a Soul to enter the child as it was born.

This worked very well, but the Souls were remembering all of their past lives, and this was leading to disruptions in the development of their psyche. It was decided that an Emissary of the Collective should be called to come to Earth, and mask the memory of the new born Soul so that it would not be able to access its previous memory. The Council of the Collective called this Emissary Gabriel.

So it was that Gabriel began to touch every child born to the Taran on Earth just below its nose, and mask the Souls memory of previous lives. This touch left a visible indentation in the Tarans face between the nose, and upper lip.

Time moved along, and soon there was a multitude of Tarans on Earth, so many that there were not enough Souls to inhabit every child born. Contact was made with the Collective to find a remedy for this problem. It was decided that Spirits of the Universe would be given the opportunity of becoming Earth Souls, and experiencing the Earth as they grew with the Taran. The stipulation being they must attain the same level of Development as all Spirits in the Collective, the same as the Tarans were bound to.

Even with the stipulation many Universal Spirits came to the Realm of Earth to be born of the Taran.

Visitation of G.O.D

ISIS the Supreme G.O.D. of a DOMA warship was given the task of conveying this information to the Tarans. ISIS visited a principal leader of the descendants of the Tarans who was called by his followers Moses. To Moses, ISIS gave ten tablets, on which were written The Collective laws.

And ISIS spoke all these words, saying: 'I am the LORD your G.O.D.

ONE: 'You shall have no other gods before Me.'

TWO: 'You shall not make for yourself a carved image--any likeness of anything that is in heaven above, or that is in the earth beneath, or that is in the water under the earth.'

THREE: 'You shall not take the name of the LORD your God in vain.'

FOUR: 'Remember the Sabbath day, to keep it holy.'

FIVE: 'Honor your father and your mother.'

SIX: 'You shall not murder.'

SEVEN: 'You shall not commit adultery.'

EIGHT: 'You shall not steal.'

NINE: 'You shall not bear false witness against your neighbor.'

TEN: 'You shall not covet your neighbor's house; you shall not covet your neighbor's wife, or his male servant, or his female servant, or his ox, or his donkey, or anything that is your neighbor's.'

ISIS gave Moses the Commandments ONE, TWO, and THREE, because the people were making Golden Idols, and then worshiping them, these 3 extra Laws were not part of the Collectives directive, but were deemed necessary to guide the Tarans in the proper direction. ISIS wanted to break this practice and giving the people these Commandments was a way of doing it.

ISIS also gave Moses a way of contacting the Council of Souls so that the Tarans of Earth could contact the Collective to seek guidance and protection from their enemies.

ISIS made it quite clear to Moses that the Collective law was to be obeyed, and those who of their own freewill followed the law would be accepted into the realm of The Collective. Those who chose not to follow the law would never be accepted into the realm.

ISIS convened a meeting of the Council of Souls, which was in the orbit of Earth, and gave them the duty of watching over the Earth beings to ensure no other Entities harmed them.

Time moved along, the 4th TM ended, and many of the Tarans on Earth had chosen not to follow the laws, and ways of The Collective.

The Collective Council met to discuss the early termination of the experiment, and the immediate acceptance of those souls that followed the laws.

The Emissary

The Council decided that the experiment would continue to its full term of 7 TM. An emissary would be sent to Earth to teach the Earth humans the WAY of the Collective, and to offer the Taran one last chance to enter the Collective.

There was much discussion about how to introduce the emissary into the world of the Taran. It was agreed the emissary's arrival should be of great Significance; so that it would be recognized the event was truly important. Some of the Council thought the emissary should descend onto Earth on a great shimmering ball of Golden light brighter than the Star of Siderious. Others argued for a less spectacular entrance for fear of frightening the people away.

The Council finally decided to send Gabriel as their representative to find a truly pure Earth female who had not mated with an Earth male. Gabriel was given a seed of the Supreme leader, G.O.D, and directed to implant the seed in the Earth female. When the child was born of the Earth woman, it would be the descendant of G.O.D, and would possess the qualities of G.O.D.

Gabriel journeyed to Earth, and after much searching found an Earth female named Mary. He appeared to Mary, and told her of the directions given by the Council. Gabriel implanted the seed of G.O.D. in Mary, and withdrew to the orbit of Earth to consult the Council of Souls.

The Earth Council of Souls agreed with the action taken by the Collective Council, but they advised Gabriel that the Tarans would forever shun the child of Mary if there were any suspicion the child had no Earth father. They advised Gabriel to return to Earth, and select an Earth father to help nurture the Emissary, and so it was that Gabriel returned to Earth in search of an Earth male to be with Mary, to act as the emissary's guardian.

Gabriel searched the Earth, and at last found a male named Joseph. Joseph obeyed the law The Collective, lived a devout life, and was of kind, gentle nature. Gabriel visited Joseph to direct him in his duties to Mary and the emissary. After this visit, Joseph took Mary as his wife.

Mary & Joseph gave the emissary the Earthly name of Jesus. He was taken to their home to live the first part of his life as part of an Earth family.

When Jesus was 18 Earth years, he traveled to the communities of Earth, learning the ways of the Earth beings, and assessing the possibilities of accepting souls other than those of Moses descendants. He found the ability to have soul, was not limited to those who were descendants of the experiment. The ability to have soul had been spread to all Earth beings.

Jesus's discovery that all Earth beings had soul was joyous news to the Collective Council. The potential Number of souls that could be harvested, and brought into the realm of The Collective would be much Greater than expected, and the power of The Collective would be greatly increased. The Collective Council decided to use the remaining TM of the experiment to recruit all the souls of Earth to the realm of the collective. They would have to learn the ways, and the Law of The Collective, Jesus would be the teacher.

Jesus returned to the land of his birth, and began his teaching mission. Progress was very slow. The Earth beings displayed very little interest in learning the ways, or laws of the Collective

Jesus consulted with the Council of the Collective and the Earth Council of Souls to seek a method to spread the teachings to all Earth people. I was decided that he should form his own Council of Earth beings that would devote their lives to The Collective, and aid in the Teaching.

Jesus chose 12 males from the Earth society, and began to teach them the Way of the Collective. They traveled throughout the land, Jesus spoke to many gatherings, telling the glory of the Collective realm, inviting the Earth beings to follow the ways of the Collective, and join him on his return to the realm.

Throughout his travels Earth beings approached him, and appealed to have others healed of maladies. Jesus did as asked, placed his hands on the inflicted being, and removed the cause of the malady. Word of this healing spread quickly and the appeals increased dramatically. Jesus empowered his Council to do the same healing, but most doubted their ability, and could not heal to the level of Jesus.

A period of four Earth years passed, and a significant number of Earth beings still had not accepted the WAY of The Collective. The Collective Council decided to return Jesus to the realm In order that he might lead the Council in preparation for the acceptance of the Earth souls. The responsibility of teaching the WAY, and laws of The Collective would be left to Jesus's Council.

To assist the Council of Jesus in their task, the Collective Council decided, Jesus's departure from Earth should be significantly spectacular enough to implant his presence and teaching of the WAY of the Collective Laws in the minds of Earth beings for all time. The departure should also serve as an example of the WAY for all Tarans to follow.

In that period of Earth time the ruling class punished those who violated their ways by a method of death called crucifixion. The one to be punished was fastened to a large cross of wood, which was stood erect so that the one being punished hung on the cross in anguish until the final expiration. This was the method of departure chosen by the Collective Council for Jesus.

The Collective Council also decided that Jesus would not simply leave after his expiration, but rather he would appear to his Council and others so that the word would spread that he died, and then returned to life.

G.O.D. concurred with the decision, Jesus was advised and the Earth Council of Souls sent emissaries in the form of invisible spirits to implant the idea in the minds of the ruling class.

When the time for his crucifixion drew near, Jesus called his Council to join him in a final meal. He advised his Council of his departure, and instructed them in ways of remembering his presence.

Jesus made a covenant with them, in which he promised that all Earth Souls who followed his teachings, and obeyed the laws of The Collective would join him in the Realm of The Collective, and dwell there for all time. One of his council asked

"Teacher, which is the greatest commandment in the Law?" Jesus replied: " 'Love the Lord your God with all your heart and with all your soul and with all your mind.' This is the first and greatest commandment. And the second is like it: 'Love your neighbor as yourself.' All the Law and the Prophets hang on these two commandments" (Matthew 22:36-40)

As Jesus and his Council departed the meeting place, the emissaries put the plan of departure in motion.

The very next morning Jesus was seized by soldiers of the ruling class, taken before the Governor of the land, and sentenced to crucifixion.

Jesus was made to carry his cross to the place of crucifixion. He then was attached to the cross by nails driven through his arms, and legs. Then the cross was erected so that the nails suspended Jesus. He remained on the cross until soldiers of the ruling class determined there was no life in his body.

This was to be the shinning example of The WAY for all Tarans to Follow. The message of the Cross-was that Jesus willingly laid down his life, because of his LOVE for the Tarans, and they should do the same for their fellow Tarans. This is the WAY of the Collective Unequivocal LOVE for all Spirits, and creations of the ONE.

His Council and followers were allowed to remove his body from the cross, and prepare it for entombment, which was the custom for Earth beings at that time. Jesus body was placed in a cave tomb, which had been provided by one of his followers. Rolling a large stone into the entrance sealed the tomb.

After Jesus's Council and followers left the area, emissaries of The Earth Council of Souls went to the tomb, revived Jesus, and ascended into the Earth's orbit. As a sign of his departure they rolled the large stone away from the entrance to the tomb.

When Jesus's followers came to the tomb for a visit they marveled at the fact he was not there, and the stone had been rolled away.

In the next three Earth days Jesus appeared to his Council, and followers in the Earth form that was his when he dwelt amongst them. All marveled at his appearance in life form, for they had witnessed his death on the cross, and his entombment.

When the time came for his final departure, Jesus appeared to his Council and bade them to spread the Word of his resurrection, and the truth that all Taran Souls who believed with him would likewise be resurrected. He then rose bodily into the orbit of Earth.

Jesus's Council was awestruck by the circumstances of his death and resurrection. Collectively they wrote the story of his coming to Earth, his life on Earth, and his final departure. They traveled the far reaches on Earth spreading this story, and the covenant he had made with them at their final meal.

The Council called Jesus "Christ" as they spread his teachings, and promise to other Tarans; the number of followers began to grow in numbers. These teachers and followers became known as "Christians".

Time For a Correction

Things have not gone as planned with the Christian Tarans; it is now 2 TM past the time of the Emissary Jesus, the Laws of the Universe, and the WAY of The Collective are blithely ignored, or at a minimum totally Forgotten.

The Council of The Collective has decided that a different course of action must be followed in order that the Earth's population of Tarans might be saved, and their Souls brought to the home worlds to occupy newly formed bodies, that have been stored while awaiting these Souls to activate them.

Souls from The Collective will be sent as replacements for the Souls of Tarans that are existence on Earth. Once in place these Souls will be able to show The WAY to other Tarans on Earth.

There is some urgency to this action because scientists of The Collective have discovered an anomaly in the orbit of the Earth around its star, which has resulted in a slight wobble in the orbit. This wobble combined with a melting of the Polar ice caps is predicted to cause a shift in the magnetic Poles of the Earth 180 degrees, resulting in the complete annihilation of the mammal species on Earth.

Tarans are the dominant species of mammal on the planet so there is great concern for their existence, and the survival of the Souls, which have been nurtured therein.

Souls in The Collective have long ago mastered the technique of freely moving out of an occupied body, and journeying to distant locations, or entering other bodies. It is this technique that will be used to replace the Souls of the Tarans.

The Souls that are nurtured in the body of the Earth beings do not have the capability of leaving the body at will. The Earth beings body must enter the state of death in order for the Soul to depart. The subject Tarans who will have their Soul replaced must therefore enter a phase of death in order that their Soul can be freed to leave the physical body, and be replaced by a Soul of the Collective.

This method of entering the Earth society was perfected after the successful time Jesus spent on Earth. The Collective required a method by which we could enter Earth society, and influence change. What better way than to assume the identity of an existing Earth being.

With the impending destruction of Earth's population the reproduction of the Taran species will also end, and there will be no further ability to nurture Souls, therefore the harvesting of Souls must take place prior to the shift in Poles.

Thus we have become more active in the number of replacements carried out. The Earth beings have noted an increase in the number of Earth bodies being resurrected, and some have questioned the happenings. We have introduced the change to the Earth Tarans as a phenomenon called "Near Death Experience". This Death and Resurrection of the Earth body is now accepted by the Earth beings as a Near Death Experience, and the increasing number of incidents is not causing alarm amongst the Tarans.

A number of us (Souls) of The Collective have been chosen to be the initial corps of replacements for the Taran Souls.

I am ZXN37 the Soul of a member of the DOMA armed forces that once fought on the side of the Elohim to save the Adamu, and ensure the existence of the Taran on Earth. My fellow corps members and I have traveled through the universe to make final preparations for the harvest of these Earthly Souls.

We have arrived in the Star system Siderious, and are proceeding to the third planet in the system, which those who are there call Earth so that we may harvest as many Souls as possible at the end of the Tarans existence.

The purpose of our arrival is to provide one last opportunity for the Earth beings to choose to obey the Laws of the Collective, and follow The WAY.

To accomplish this task we will enter the body of chosen ones. The Souls of the chosen ones will immediately be taken to the Realm of the Collective for transformation.

At the time of our arrival in Earth orbit, the number of Earth beings referred to as Christians, has increased dramatically. More than one third of the Earths population is called Christian, most believe in the presence of Jesus on Earth, but many do not obey the laws of The Collective.

There are many others in the remaining two thirds of the Taran population that are aware of the Law of the Universe, but do not follow The WAY, these Tarans will also be given the opportunity of joining with the Souls of The Collective. The Collective have sent Emissaries to these beings as well, so they are well aware of the Law, and The WAY.

The Chosen Ones are of male and female Earth beings. The sign of their choosing is the same as that of Jesus. The seed of Collective Humans was implanted to an Earth female who had not been with an Earth male. The Chosen Ones are the first born of these Earth females. Many of the Earth females have birthed other Earth beings, but only the first-born are the Chosen Ones.

The Chosen Ones have been prompted to live outside the Law of the Universe, and not follow The WAY. Thus their associates on Earth know them as wanderers, and transgressors.

After the Near Death Experience we of The Collective live the Earth life as we have existed in the Collective. The result is a dramatic change in the way a resurrected Earth body behaves.

The Earth beings relative to the Chosen One, marvel at the change. The change explained by the telling of the Experience and the enlightenment gained while in the state of death. The complete reversal of behavior also creates an opportunity to teach The Law of the Universe, and The WAY of The Collective

Those Earth beings that listen, and learn from the Chosen One are said to do so, because the Chosen One "Has seen the Light, and the coming of the Glory".

One of the more successful Chosen Ones on the eve of his departure from the Earth sphere said to his followers: "Do not weep for me, for I have seen the Glory of the Lord. I have seen the Promised Land". Shortly thereafter his life on Earth was terminated, and he returned to the Realm of The Collective.

To this time the Chosen is shown on their media, and his Word is broadcast throughout the Earth. If only all of the Chosen Ones could be so successful, and have the Earth Tarans follow their example, the harvest of Souls would be successful beyond the Council of The Collective's wildest expectations.

Those of us that are to replace chosen ones must now prepare ourselves for the task at hand. The transformation from being able to move about the Universe freely, to being solidly in one place can be overwhelming.

To begin the process we must observe the chosen one in its earth environment so we can continue to behave as the chosen one, and there will be no indication that a replacement has occurred.

The journey from our vessel to the surface of earth is short, and I can now move around at will. It is amazing how many other Souls are present on the earth sphere. I thought all of the departed Souls dwelled in the orbit of earth, but now I see great masses of spirits are here on the surface. The Souls seem to take great pleasure in observing the Earth's inhabitants as they go about their tasks.

I am telepathically directed to my chosen one who lives in the northern hemisphere of earth. The only information I have about it, tells me that it is directly descended from one of Jesus's council, and has been on earth for 59 earth years.

Upon arrival in the presence of It, I find there are other Souls in the area who are closely aligned with it. These other Souls communicate that they have been assisting the chosen one in following a path of helping other earth beings maintain their health. Many of these Souls are also descendants of one of Jesus's council.

I am told the chosen one is James, a male Taran who is re-discovering the healing art as was taught by Jesus. He has also begun to ponder the ways of The Collective.

I find James in what appears to be a tomb, the walls are solid with no openings, and the top is also solid. There is a door on the one end that leads out into another closed area

The other end is a room where Tarans deposit their waste. The spirits communicate, advising me that it has been ordained "James must stay in these surroundings an indeterminate time, studying, writing the story of the chosen ones, and preparing to aid the Tarans in choosing the Way of The Collective at the final harvesting."

So be it! My chosen one spends its lifetime imprisoned in a tomb, surrounded by learning instruments, and I must replace It, allow It to journey to the Realm of The Collective, and complete freedom.

The spirits communicate that James has already had a "Near Death Experience" brought about by his style of living out his earth existence. James's Soul left the body, but was returned at the direction of the Earth Council.

My mission as James is to remain on earth until the last of the souls is harvested. I must publish the story of The Collective, and help as many souls as possible choose The WAY.

The Life of James

The mind banks of the chosen ones contain the information we require to fit into earth civilization, and we must absorb all of this information during the replacement process.

I must learn of James's existence here on earth. James has a room in this building, apart from the tomb that he uses to communicate with the spirits. There will be no need to return to my vessel to make the transformation; we will use James's room.

We have chosen an Earth Sabbath to make the transformation, because James has another Earth being in the tomb to carry out his duties.

We enter the room which James calls his studio. There is a circle of Earth stones around the perimeter of the room. In the center there is a stand large enough that James can lay down on it. Underneath the stand is an earth crystal mounted on an earth stone.

James secures the door to the studio, and then burns incense to cleanse the atmosphere. His helping spirits gather at the edge of the stone circle, and James lays down on the stand.

I approach James as he lies on the stand, and gently touch his forehead. James is aware of my presence, we communicate freely, I make James aware of the transformation that is at hand, and I begin reading the life files of his memory bank.

James Mother Ruth was an unmarried descendant of a member of Jesus's Council called "James". Her family had assumed the name Calvary as a sign of their association with the Resurrection of Jesus.

Jesus was said to have died on the cross at Calvary, over time other Tarans persecuted the followers of Jesus, and the family changed the spelling of the name. The family was then known as Calvert.

In Ruth's 22nd year an Emissary visited her, and inseminated her with the seed of a Member of the Council of The Collective The Emissary communicated with Ruth, told her of the coming glory, and entrusted her to raise the chosen one for It's final destiny.

Ruth was struck with fear, and loathing by the visit of the Emissary, she was working as a housekeeper for a woman named Thelma who was quite ill. Her feelings led her to confide in the woman. At first the two women thought Ruth was dreaming about the Emissary's visit, but as time passed it became obvious that Ruth was indeed with child.

So it came to pass that the infant male was born in the spring of the next year. He was given the name Robert Louis Calvert.

Ruth did not want the infant, because it would not fit in her lifestyle, and would restrict her ability to earn a living. Ruth's mother came to the hospital where the infant had been born, and took the infant to her home to be raised. Ruth left for another land to earn her living.

Robert was cared for by his grandmother, and 3 aunts, and knew nothing of his mother.

Two and a half Earth years after his birth Robert's mother married, and with her husband decided to raise Robert as their own. Robert was taken from his Grandmother's home, and moved to the home of Ruth and her husband James.

Ruth and her husband James adopted Robert, and his name was changed to James Robert Louis Williams.

As I read the life files of James's memories I find that the stigma of having been born to an unwed mother has followed him all the days of his life, He has been known to his adopted families as "Ruth's little bastard".

As I read the files I also discover that James has led a life that would see him referred to in earth terms as "Miserable Bastard", but he has begun to change since his first transformation, and the stage is set so that I may assume his life without any of his family, or associates questioning the change in personality.

Finally the reading is over, and James's Soul is allowed to leave his Taran body, we exchange a brief moment then he is gone to the mother ship, and his journey to The Collective.

Now I enter James's earthly body. I am James, and I must accomplish my mission, and prepare as many Souls as possible for the harvest.

The Mission Begins

I return to the tomb, which I am aware is called a "Monitoring Station" it is used to receive signals from security devices that are installed in premises throughout the area.

This is a very gloomy place to be shut in. The only contact with the outside world is by means of electronic devices. There are 2 primitive learning units in the room, one of which is designated to answer incoming alarm calls, and the other one has been used strictly as a backup to the first one.

It is not hard to accomplish the monitoring, the reports from the Security Systems are few, and there are long stretches of inactivity. I am bored with this existence shortly after I arrive here.

I get the urge to explore the community in which the Monitoring Station is located, decide to leave James body, and go have a look around. I lay James down on a cot in the Monitoring Station, away I go out of his body, up and away high above the city.

There are many lighted areas I can see, there are primitive vehicles going to and fro, but they are limited to travel on the surface only. I can see these vehicles emit a sort of fog that eventually gathers high above the city.

Off in the distance I see a vessel in the air that appears to be able to travel high above the land surface. I move to have a closer look at this vessel, and find that it too emits a fog as it travel through the air.

Suddenly I am being summonsed by the other Souls that are in the proximity. "Get back to James" I don't know what the urgency is, but I go back into the Monitoring Station, James is right where I left him, but somehow the body does not seem right.

I re-enter James's body only to find it cold and lifeless. "Breathe" "Breathe" I can hear the other Souls communicating, and then I remember in the mind files there is an automatic function of the Taran body that brings air in, and expels it. Once I have breathed in and out a couple of times I can feel life coming back into James's body.

I have just learned that the Taran body is not capable of functioning without the Soul being present. I now realize that I must take in energy physically to keep James's body functioning normally.

A representative of the Earth Council of Souls visits me. The representative advises me of rules to be followed during my stay with James as his Soul, and life Essence.

First Rule:

Never leave the Taran body unless it is left in a sacred space specifically blessed for that purpose. (For example the Studio) The body might even be left outside if there was a place prepared for it to rest, but the body was not to just be left lying around anywhere it might be convenient.

Second Rule:

YOU have to live the life as the subject Taran would have lived the life. Make no sudden changes in the Tarans behavior.

Third Rule;

Use only the Tarans intelligence level. Do not exhibit the knowledge of the Collective until the proper avenue has been found to release the knowledge.

<u>Fourth Rule:</u>

Do nothing that will arouse the suspicions of other Tarans that are acquainted with James. No Taran must know of James's transition until the proper time, as decided by the Council of the Collective.

Learning

Fine now that I know the rules I can get on with my mission. I turn on the second learning device, and find that it is connected to what the Tarans call "The Internet". It appears that this Internet is a wide spread network of Tarans that connects through a series of locations specifically designed for learning, and sharing information.

The learning device has to be operated manually; the input is through a keyboard that one uses to spell out their message. The Tarans call these devices "Computers", they function much like the Terminals on the home world, except the home world terminals are controlled telepathically. It will take me a while to get used to this method of using the computer.

I find a communication entity called "Hotmail", and decide to enroll in the service. I fill in all the necessary documentation, it asks for a user name, so I enter ZXN, and send the enrollment request. Seconds later I receive a message on the screen that ZXN is unacceptable as a user name, because usernames must contain a minimum of 4 letters or numbers. I will try ZXN37, which is my designation, and the series of my joining the DOMA forces. I re send the enrollment request and receive an instant confirmation of approval.

From here on until the end of my time on Earth I will be known as ZXN37.

As I explore the Internet I find many interesting "Chat Rooms" these are places where Tarans of many different interests go to talk to one another. There are many interests listed in the directory to these rooms. There is one called Inter Stellar Travelers that seemed to be something I would be interested in.

I entered the chat room, and was immediately greeted by many of the participants," what a friendly group" I thought. As I observed their conversation a realization soon came to me that these Tarans were totally unaware of any kind of stellar travel. Disappointed I left the chat room to continue my search for learning possibilities.

The intelligence level of the Tarans using the Internet seemed to be on a very primitive level, so I signed off, and decided to explore some of James's reading material.

Many of James books were about healing the Taran body, and the energies that exist to cause deficiencies in the Taran health. James had taken many courses to learn about the Taran body and how to keep the body in relatively good condition. James also learned the Taran mind had much to do with the maintenance of Taran health.

I was interrupted in my reading by the ringing of the doorbell; someone wanted to visit the Monitoring Station. I remembered the procedure from James's mind file, and used the intercom to ask who was there.

It was Johanna who was at the door. A quick search of the mind files identified her as one of James associates, so I pushed the buttons that would open the door, and allow her entrance to the Monitoring Station.

Johanna is a lovely young lady that is a special friend of James as well as an associate healer. We soon were immersed in a spirited conversation regarding the different methods of balancing energies in the Taran body. Johanna also performs what the Tarans know as 'Therapeutic

Massage" which the practitioner uses to cause relaxation, and healing in the Taran body.

Johanna is here to operate the Monitoring Station in order that I may go to James's home, and relax. I cannot tell her that I do not require relaxation, so I agree to leave the Monitoring Station.

Outside I find a blue vehicle, which I know is James's, it is an odd looking contraption compared to the ones on the home world, but I decide to make use of it if I can. I enter the vehicle, and put the key in the hole made for it. When I turn the key I can hear the motor start.

I discover a lever marked R, N, Dr1, & Dr2, and when I move it to R. the vehicle begins to move backwards. I find a pedal that makes the vehicle stop, then move the lever to Dr1, the vehicle moves forward, and I find I can control its direction by turning a wheel that is in front of my seat. I make it away from James's building, and out on to a large pathway that I sense leads to his home.

I guide the vehicle out on to this large pathway, and let it carry me along with all the other vehicles on the pathway. There are a lot of friendly Tarans on the pathway, and they salute me as they pass by extending the middle finger of their hand, and pumping it up and down. I can see some of them verbally greeting me, but I cannot hear what they are saying. I return their one finger salute, which in turn gets them to react vigorously, and become more animated in their salutes.

As I proceed up the pathway a red vehicle similar in shape to my vehicle suddenly pulls in front of me, and stops. I step on the petal that makes my vehicle stop and avoid running into the stopped vehicle.

A large Taran exits the stopped vehicle from the left side, and an even larger Taran exits the stopped vehicle from the Right side. I must be friendly to these Tarans so I exit my vehicle, and move to meet them. "You Fucking Old Son of a Bitch we will have to teach you a lesson" says the one who exited the stopped vehicle on the left side. I always like to learn, but this Taran does not seem friendly, nor does the other one.

I see the other Taran has some sort of a stick in his hand, something in my mind file says that it is a baseball bat. It occurs to me that we are not about to have a friendly chat, and there is a lot of hostility coming from these Tarans.

I telepathically order the Taran with the baseball bat to apply it on the head of the other Taran, which he does with some gusto. The bat wielding Taran sees his associate crumple to the surface of the pathway, and immediately drops his baseball bat. There is a lot of blood coming out the ears of the Taran who got hit. His associate is now over at the side of the pathway, I can see his body convulsing, and fluid coming out of his mouth.

I examine the first Taran, and see that his brain has been flopped around inside his head from the blow he suffered. I take his head in my hands, and use my mind power to restore his brain to its original configuration. The Taran opens his eyes, and stares dumbly in my direction. His brain is restored, but it seems some of the knowledge cells are scrambled. I call to the other Taran, and tell him he should get his friend to a healing place.

I help the second Taran lift the injured Taran into the back of his vehicle, the other Taran runs to the left side of the vehicle, jumps in, and roars off down the pathway.

As they are leaving I realize that a large crowd of Tarans has gathered to watch the confrontation. I see a white vehicle with Red & Blue flashing lights come to a stop on the opposite side of the pathway. I instinctively know that this is a Police Taran. The Police Taran exits his vehicle, and makes his way towards me. "Is this your vehicle?" he asks as he points to James's vehicle. "Yes" I answer. "Get this piece of Shit moving then, and quit blocking traffic," he says. I get into the vehicle, and start moving up the pathway again. The next thing I know the vehicle with the flashing Red & Blue lights is in front of me, and stopping. The Police Taran gets out of his vehicle, and comes to my vehicle.

He is mouthing something, but I can't hear what he is saying, because of the loud noise coming from my vehicle. I turn the key to off, and the noise stops. The Police Taran's face is turning Red, I find a handle that lowers the window in my door, and at last I can hear the Police Taran.

"Where in the Fuck did you learn to drive you stupid old fart?" he is very loudly speaking. I do not know what he is talking about; I thought I was doing wonderfully well going along the pathway. Maybe if I levitated the vehicle, and proceeded a little faster toward James's house, that would please this Police Taran. Something tells me that this would be a violation of Rule #2, but what the heck I already blew it on the other Tarans. I use my mind power, and levitate the vehicle away from the Police Taran; I look back, and see him standing on the pathway apparently frozen in place.

I proceed to another pathway, which I know by instinct is James home pathway, and guide the vehicle to the surface in front of James's house. I realize that I have a lot to learn about the customs, and habits of the Tarans.

Home

I proceed up the path leading to the house. I wonder what surprises await me inside. The door is unlocked so I step inside; "Hello" I hear a pleasant voice call, so I answer back.

A pleasant looking woman with graying hair appears, and begins to tell me about people I assume are acquaintances of hers & James. I understand that she is James's wife Anne. Anne hands me a cup of coffee, I sit down at the table, and listen while she tells me about her days since I was last home. It seems the little dog is not healthy, and the cats messed up on the floor, the garage door needs fixing, and the lawnmower needs sharpening.

I am not ready to do any physical work on this planet, but I find some tools and manage to get the garage door operating. Then I manage to remove the blade from the lawnmower, do the best I can at grinding some of the dents out of it, and get it back on the lawnmower. This has been a tiring adventure, I think I will go and rest up a bit, but no; "We have to go to Wal Mart" Anne informs me. I pretend I know exactly what she is talking about.

Out to the little red vehicle that is parked in front of the one I brought over here. Anne goes around on the left side and opens the doors, it is a good thing she is going to drive, and I can watch and learn by watching her. She puts the key in the hole, turns it; I can hear the motor start same as the other one, and then she moves the lever to make the vehicle move. Anne has her right foot on the small pedal next to the Stopping pedal, the more she pushes on it the faster we go, so now I have learned something useful, and I can probably make the other vehicle move the same way.

Wal Mart is packed with Tarans of all shapes, sizes, and colors. Most of them are very rude, pushing little wire baskets into each other, and uttering sounds that sound like a beast growling.

We go to the pet food area, Anne picks up a whole bunch of tins, puts them in our wire basket, and then indicates that I should load 2 boxes of something called clumping cat litter into our basket. I start to pick up the first box, soon realize I need 2 hands, and some effort to get the box into the wire basket.

After I have the 2 boxes loaded, we proceed around the building, I think Anne is looking at everything in the store; I just want to get out of the place, and go back to the Monitoring Station. Finally we go up to place where all the Tarans are lined up and I realize this is where you have to pay for the stuff in your basket.

I get in line to get the stuff in our basket checked through, there are 10 or 12 Tarans with baskets in front of me, so I decide to be patient, and observe the Tarans around me. There is a big round female behind me in the line; she keeps bumping her basket into the back of my legs. I try to be patient, but she insists on pounding the back of my legs with the basket. Finally I can take no more of her antics; I concentrate on seeing her peeing on the floor, and sure enough only a short time later the legs of her clothing are starting to get wet. She lets out a horrible shriek, leaves her cart, and then I see her running towards a sign that says "Washrooms". I go through the checkout, Anne pays for the stuff, and we leave.

Back at Anne & James house I find my way to the bedroom, lay down, and rest for the remaining part of time I have left before going back to the Monitoring station.

It is dark when I leave for the monitoring station, I manage to find the switch for the lights, I get the go stick in Dr1, and then step hard on the little petal beside the stop pedal, Wow did I get that vehicle moving, there was a cloud of blue smoke hanging in the place where I had been stopped. I manage to regulate the speed of the vehicle down to where all the other vehicles were traveling on the pathways. No one is showing me greeting signs like they did when I was on my way over to the house.

I make it back to the Monitoring station without incurring the wrath of any Tarans, and feel greatly relieved to be back inside the quiet confines of the station. Johanna has let me in, it is her turn to go out and go to her house, but I sense reluctance on her part. "How about a cup of tea" she asks, and I tell her that would be ok.

I want to get back to the Internet, and continue my learning, but I sense Johanna would like to stay and talk for a while. I ask her about the middle finger greeting I received when I was on my way to James's house. She laughs and tells me that is the way people insult you, it means "Up Your Ass". Oh ok; I can understand why people got so agitated when I greeted them back. We have our tea, and then Johanna leaves to go home.

Back to the Task

Once I am alone in the Monitoring Station I am able to turn the Internet on, and resume searching for intelligent Tarans who are using the system to learn of other worlds, and beings. I must first learn the level that their discussions have reached, so I find a heading in the discussion rooms that reads "Spirituality", and decide to visit the rooms to see what knowledge is being imparted.

There are many rooms under this heading, and 90% are headed in the name of a Religion Like; the Evangelical Church for example. A visit to some of these rooms soon brings the realization that they are espousing their own form of Spirituality, and each Religious group has their own idea of what Spirituality means. I enter a couple of the rooms, and observe the conversations, sometimes I am asked for my input, and I ask "What part of your Spirituality recognizes the Laws of the Universe (Ten Commandments) or the WAY as per the teachings of Jesus". I am told that Jesus did away with the Ten Commandments, and taught they only had to believe in him. Somehow I don't think this is what he taught, but I say nothing, and excuse myself from the room.

The reason I said nothing in response to their answers is the fact they have been fully indoctrinated in their beliefs, to contradict them would start a huge fuss, and that is not my mission. I will leave the lessons of what is to come at the end of Earth's time to change the minds of those who have been indoctrinated by the Religions.

Eventually I find a room that is titled "Spirits of the Universe" which sounds more like the discussion group I am looking for. Upon entering the room I am greeted by all that are in attendance, made to feel at home, and invited to join in on the conversation. I advise all that I am new to the discussion rooms, and would like to observe the conversation before joining in. This is acceptable to the supervisors, their conversations resume, and I begin to observe.

Most of the conversation centers around the ability to contact departed Spirits after they have left the earthly body. I was not aware that Tarans had this ability, so I listen intently to the conversation. There are also Tarans that tell of being able to read the record of past lives that a Spirit has experienced. Indeed there are all sorts of talented Tarans in this room.

"What sort of Spirituality do you follow ZXN37?" a moderator asks. Not being accustomed to answering that sort of question, I hesitate for a moment trying to draft an answer that won't upset the room. I tell them that I follow the Law of the Universe, and the WAY in an attempt to have my own Spirit developed to the highest level of Humankind, but I have not developed the talents that they apparently have. I am told they hold seminars, and teach methods to develop these talents. I express and interest, and am given a schedule of times that the seminars would be held.

One of the moderators' signals they wish to have a private chat with me, so I answer the signal. "We do not discuss Religion in this room ZXN37!" I didn't think I was saying anything about Religion, just that I follow the Law of the Universe. The Moderator advises me, "We do not speak of such things in this room ZXN37, and if you do speak of it again you will be banished from the room."

This room does not seem to be what I am looking for so I say goodbye and leave to once again search for someone on Earth that follows the Law given to Moses, and follow the WAY of Jesus.

I am about to turn the Internet off when I see a heading "Native

Spirituality". I decide to check some of the rooms under that heading. I find one "Shamanism" that has a notation "Come and join us for a discussion on contacting your Spirit Guides" this sounds very interesting so I enter the room.

The room is full of Tarans with strange nicknames, I soon learn that Native Americans name their children after different elements in the nature of Earth "Running Rabbit, Bright Moon, Standing Bear, Creek Runs Dry, and on, and on".

They are having a lively discussion about being able to contact their departed ancestor's Spirits, some say they enter into a state of semi-consciousness, and then are able to speak to the ancestors. Others dance for long times to have a vision of the ancestors. All speak reverently of their ancestors, and the lessons that can be learned from them.

I am contacted on the side by one of the moderators, to have a private chat. I enter the private chat room with some apprehension of being banished from the room. "Do you follow the Shamanic Path?' the moderator asks. "I am not aware of the Shamanic Path!' I tell him. 'You are a white man then!" he says 'No matter all who are willing to learn our ways are welcome to be with us" "What if I tell you I follow the Law of the Universe, will I be banished from the room?' I ask. "Certainly not, we all follow the Law!' he says, "Why would you think you should be banished for speaking of the law?' I tell him that I have been told that to speak of the Law of the Universe is to discuss Religion. "LMAO" he replies. I am really uncertain what he means, and am hesitant to show my ignorance by asking him. He indicates we should rejoin the main room, and closes the chat.

Back in the main room I see others using strange phrases, and soon learn these are abbreviations for expressions. I am given a location where I can learn what all the abbreviations mean. I go to the location, and find a complete listing of all the abbreviations. LMAO means Laugh My Ass Off, my oh my I would like to see that happen, but I guess he was just speaking figuratively.

Back in the Shamanism room I find many interesting stories being told about contact that has been made with Spirits in the Realm of

Earth. I learn that the Spirits have long ago conveyed the Laws of the Universe to the Native people of Earth. The Spirits have also taught the people that their Spirits (Souls) will rejoin the Great Spirit, and the Creator once their physical life on Earth is completed if they live by the Law.

These teachings are so similar to those of The Collective I get the urge to step in, and tell all there is to tell about The Collective, but I am restrained by a telepathic order not to intervene in the beliefs of these people. I listen intently though, as many different lessons are discussed. Many of these lessons are received by mind picture stories that are called "Visions". In order to have a vision many of these people follow a strict regime of not eating for a period of 7 Earth days before they go seeking a vision, they call this act a "Vision Quest". I am really anxious to try to experience a Vision Quest. I leave the room, and turn off the computer.

There is a book in James library titled "The Celtic Shaman" I take it down, and start reading. This is a very interesting book that tells how to "Journey" to the Lower, and Upper worlds. It seems the Celtic Shaman uses the Journey much like the Native people use the Vision Quest. I understand that James had been following the teachings in the Celtic Shaman book for quite sometime. I decide when next I am relieved I will go to James's studio, and try my hand at journeying.

Sometime later the doorbell rings, and a male identifies himself as Garth, a quick search of the mind files tells me this is James's step-son, and he has come to relieve me. I let Garth in, and exchange pleasantries with him. Then I am able to leave, and make my way to the studio.

Journeying

The studio is a room that is in the center of the building, completely enclosed, having no windows, and only one entrance port. There is a circle of stones, with a gray bench in the center of the circle; underneath the bench there is a large stone with an earth crystal mounted on it. The walls of the studio are painted a very light green color, there is a shelf attached to 3 sides of the room, and on the shelf there are several items, which are used in the preparation for, and the performance of the Journey.

One of the items is a recording device with a recording in it, when I get the recording tape out of the device; I find the notation "Visit to the Dark Goddess" inscribed on the label of the tape. This must be one of the Journeys that James has gone on.

The smudge dish is readily identifiable due to it being covered with ashes. I find a vial with a kind of soft material in it; one sniff of the contents tells my memory banks that it is the one James has been using. I place a small amount of the smudge on the dish, find a match, and light the smudge. The smudge smolders, and emits a plume of smoke, which I understand is the cleansing element for the circle that must be used before each Journey.

I will follow the ritual that was contained in the Celtic Shaman book:

To the East, and Spring, and Air, while facing in the Easterly direction, and wafting the smoke.

To the South, and Summer, and Fire while facing the South, and wafting the smoke.

To the West, and Autumn, and Water while facing West, and wafting the smoke

To the North, and Winter, and Death, and Renewal while facing North, and wafting the smoke.

Then to the Center of the Circle, and waft the smoke to the ground asking the Goddesses of the Earth to be with me in my journey,

Then to the Above, and asking the Blessing of the ONE, to allow me this journey.

Then wafting the smoke around the Circle asking the Spirits of the departed ancestors to be with me, and protect me while I journey.

Once the smudging is finished I lay down on the gray bench, a feeling of absolute calm comes over my being, and I manage to get the tape recorder to play; I can feel the Spirits of the Circle joining me in the Journey.

It says! We are in a peaceful room with the intent to journey to the Dark Goddess, there is a door in the side of the room that is opening, we feel our Spirits rise, and go towards the door. Once through the door there is a stairway descending in to the depths, on the right side of the stairwell there is a multi colored rope, Black, Red, and White, the rope is mounted on the wall by Gold pins with dragon heads holding the rope in their mouths.

Down the stairs we go, and soon are in a dimly lit room, once again the lights are held by dragon like fixtures with the light coming from their eyes. We are led to a dark pool of water, and told to gaze into the pool to see the reflection of what we are.

I look at the surface of the pool, and see a warrior holding 5 poison spears in his right hand, and a very large broadsword in his left, the only garment he has on is a scabbard belt meant to house the sword. The warrior's body is covered with black, red, and white paint. I am left to wonder what this means, because the tape recording prompts me to move along around the pool always going to the right.

As I move around the pool I see a figure dressed in a black shroud that flowed all the way to the floor, her head is covered, but I instantly know this is the Dark Goddess. The tape recording prompts me to approach the Dark Goddess, and present her with a gift. I search my mind banks, but realize that I have nothing physical that I can give the Goddess. There is only one thing that comes to mind is LOVE, I can give her my unequivocal LOVE. The Goddess accepts my gift, and gives me a large broadsword with jewels imbedded in the hilt; I am told this is the symbol of my earthly ancestors.

It is time to return to reality, and we are directed to the bottom of the stairs, the stairs rise towards the door that I know is on the side of the studio. Once at the door we are prompted to regain our body's presence, and return to normal reality.

I wonder at the gift that the Dark Goddess gave me, and why it would be a broadsword, am I to do battle again, or does it represent the written word, which is said to be more powerful that the sturdiest broadsword. I rise from the bench still feeling in awe of having such a vivid journey.

Later when I go back to the Monitoring Station, I find a book lying on the floor, when I pick it up the title reads "The Celtic Way". Oh another Way! I read the book, it tells of the Celtic people, and how they lived. There is also a vivid description of their warriors, it seems that men & women of the Celtic culture were considered equal, and served side by side in the Celtic armies. The Celtic warrior carried 5 poison spears in the right hand, and a broadsword in the left hand. They wore no garments except for a scabbard belt, which the broadsword could be stored in. They painted the body with black, red, and white paint just like the warrior I saw in my journey.

The reason they wore no garments was that they believed when the body died their Spirits left the body went to a special place with all the other Spirits, and then could be reborn in an infant at some later time. Consequently they believed they should leave the body naked, as it was when they were born.

Catastrophe

I turn on the computer, and to my utter disbelief the screen is blank. What could have happened to erase everything in the computers memory, there is just a blank screen with a little cursor on the upper left corner. All my information, and thoughts are gone, the teaching that I had been following, everything gone. I find Garth's phone number in the phone directory, and phone him. "What happened to the computer the screen is blank?" I ask him. "I tried to download a program that was 750 MB, then I found out that the hard drive was only 500 MB, the new program started erasing all that was on the hard drive to make room for the downloaded program, it couldn't get enough room, so the whole thing crashed."

It is a good thing that stupidity is not a good reason to kill a Taran, or Garth would have been terminated with malice at that point in time. I thank him for the information, and hang the phone up.

I stare dumbly at the blank screen, and wonder what I can do to remedy the situation, and then in a moment of realization I think about the learning terminals back on Sirius B, the parts are interchangeable. I take the cover off the useless computer, and find the hard drive, undo the screws holding it in, unplug the wiring harness, and take the hard drive out of the computer. I see a setting on the end that has Master, and Slave as the settings. I move the settings to Slave, then remove the cover of the Monitoring computer. I can see there is an extra slot in the Monitoring computer so I put the Slave hard drive in that slot, and plug it in. I close the Monitoring software, and go to the prompt that appears on the screen. Entering :// format D: causes the computer to start whirring, and making all sorts of noises, as the format of the Slave disk is configured. The screen then indicates that the formatting is complete. I re-enter the monitoring program, and remove the Slave hard drive from the computer.

I re-install the Slave hard drive in the learning computer after I have selected Master on its configuration. When the computer is turned on the C: prompt is showing on the screen, I dig out all of the program disks that were originally installed on the computer, then one by one I re-install them. The last program that is installed is the Internet program. The whole process consumed most of a day in Earth time.

Now I turn on the computer, and expect to see Internet Explorer appear on the screen, to my absolute amazement a Red screen appears with the words "Avatar Search Engine of the Occult" written in big bold letters on the screen. What the heck! I don't want anything from the occult, but I can't seem to get the computer to leave the site. I look under the heading "Books" and I find many books on Shamanism that are on James's shelves.

I had searched the word "Elohim" on the standard search engines, and received many hundreds of answers, so I wondered how many the occult would give me. I typed the word "Elohim" in the Search window, and hit enter expecting to see many answers. There was one answer, "Unbelievable" I clicked on the page and was taken immediately to "THE WAY"**. The opening page had the Double Helix symbol of the DOMA, which I readily recognized; the index showed there were 16 chapters that described different actions taken by the DOMA. Wow every Taran on Earth should read this book, and come to know their history. I printed the book off, and placed it in a large binder with the intention of sharing it with anyone who would read it, then think about the information it contained. When I put the book in the binder I made a huge mistake, the copy was in the binder so that it had to be read from right to left. Tarans have their books read from left to right. I later learned that a prophet had told the Tarans "All Holy books should be read from Right to Left". Maybe it was not such a big mistake after all!

** http://web.archive.org/web/20010815022316/www.webcom.com/ way/the-way.html

Exploring

Now that the Internet is up and running again it is time to start learning about the Earth's population, and habits so it will be apparent which Souls will be more advanced, and ready to become members of the Human society on Sirius B. It is apparent that the White or Caucasian race is the most numerous, dominant race on the planet, and is in control of most Governments. The whites are followed closely by the Yellow race, which also has large numbers of Tarans, but is only dominate in about 1/5 of the planet. The Black race covers one continent that of Africa, but their influence is spreading throughout the Planet.

The Browns are mainly in the center of a large continent, with the Yellows to the Right or East of them, and the Blacks to the Left or West of them, the Brown population is rising to equal that of the yellows. The Red race is found primarily in what is known as North America, but they are not dominant, long ago the Whites came to North America, and conquered the Red race. The Whites forced the Reds to live in certain areas of the country that are called Reservations.

Many of the Whites are very bigoted, and disdain contact with the other races; there is a sense of superiority amongst this race. Often they refer to the other races in very derogatory terms, which are very demeaning to the others. They call the blacks "Niggers, Motherfuckers", and many other unfathomable names. The Yellows they call "Chinks, Slant eyes", the Browns are "Rag heads, Pakis", but the worst is left for the Red race, or Native North Americans, who are called "Dirty Filthy Indians, Savages, Wagon burners, and Reserve rats".

I have contact with many of the races throughout my studies, the Blacks are beginning to take up the Whites bigoted ways, and refer to the other races in derogatory ways. The Yellows and Browns do not seem to use any derogatory words to describe other races.

One of the Yellows that I have close personal contacts with tells me that all people are the same, and have same kind of Souls. This attitude seems to exist throughout the whole of the Yellow race.

The Reds are the most humble of people, but they too have derogatory expressions when it comes to the Whites, but this stems from their being pushed from the land, and made to live under very restrictive conditions for a long time, while being supervised by many overbearing, abusive White men.

The Whites also introduced their Religion to the Red people, and made the Red children attend Reservation schools where the children were not allowed to speak their own language, and were indoctrinated with the White values, and Religion. Many of these children were also dreadfully abused in the schools. The older Red people that did not accept the Whites Religion and ways were said to be Heathens, and backward people.

There are many young Red people on the Internet that yearn to learn the "Old Ways", they gather in what are called "Native Chat Rooms", and discuss many issues pertaining to the Spirit, and living with the Universe.

I find one chat room especially interesting "Cherokee Eagles Nest Landing" is a room that all people of any color are welcomed, there is an adjoining web site, where all are invited to write the stories of their Tribe, or Family. People from all over the Earth come to this chat room, and share their stories. The founder of the room is called away to a different duty, and asks ZXN37 to moderate the room.

I take up the task of moderating the room with some hesitation, but soon am immersed in the many interesting conversations. There are many in the room that believe they should follow the Laws of the Universe, and show Unconditional love to all of Creation. They call the ONE "The Creator", and show great reverence to It.

One session a Person who called herself "Moon Teacher" came into the room, and dominated a discussion about Spirits, and the Spirit World. Many of the other participants in the room were draw into the conversation, stories were told of encounters with Spirits, and how sometimes the Spirits served to guide people when they were at a low point in their lives. The Spiritual encounters also served to reinforce the belief in the keeping of the Law of the Universe, and following the WAY showing Unconditional Love to all Creation.

One evening "Moon Teacher" mentioned that she would be holding Seminars on how to move one's Spirit out of the physical body, and travel anywhere in the Universe at will. She gave the address of her web site, and invited all interested people to join her.

I went to the web site, and found that anyone could join her seminars so long as they had a credit card, and paid a $50.00 entrance fee. Wow! The idea that a Spirit had to pay to learn how to leave the Taran body was quite unexpected, and I was quite taken aback, that one should be able to charge for teaching what was an integral part of the Spirit World. There were 22 people signed on for the next Seminar, I dug around and found one of James's credit cards then joined the list for the Seminar.

At the appointed time for the Seminar I turned on the computer, went on the Internet, and entered into the chat room at "Moon Teacher's" web site. It wasn't long before all the participants that had signed up for the Seminar were present and accounted for.

"Moon Teacher" entered the chat room, began by telling us all to sit quietly in front of our computers, and concentrate on what she was typing on the screen.

"Tonight we are going to the Moon, our bodies are all sitting quietly in a relaxed position in front of the computer, our hands are resting on our knees.

As you read my words on the screen I want you to see your Spirit slowly lifting out of your bodies, and positioning itself up above your head, concentrate really hard, you can see your body below you safe, and protected sitting in front of the computer. Now then move your Spirit up and away from you room up into the sky high above the Earth, you can see your house far down below you, and you are free.

Now see the moon shining ever so brightly farther up in the sky, join me as we travel up and out towards the moon. Out and out we go until at last we are above the moon's surface; look back and you can see Earth shimmering in the light of the Sun. The Earth is bright blue with white clouds drifting over it. Experience the weightlessness of being out in the Universe, and the feeling of absolute freedom.

Now we must turn our attention to returning to the body, so back to Earth we go each to their own part of the Planet, as you return to your area, feel the closeness of your body, and go to where your body is. Down into your room, then rest just above your body, now slowly slip back into your body, and feel the warmth of the room. Come back to being fully awake and in your body."

Finally "Moon Teacher" asks all participants to write about their experience with the out of body Seminar, and post it on the message board of her website. I am aghast! A ten minute reading of typing on the computer screen for $50.00, and we are supposed to write of our experiences. Many of the participants are openly enthusiastic about the Experience they had, and begin telling stories of the lights that were seen, the satellites that were orbiting earth, and some of the planets that seemed so close they could touch them. I experience none of these events, and seemed to stay rooted in my chair even though I have the ability to leave James body any time I feel the necessity.

Back in Cherokee Eagles Nest Landing, I see there is a discussion about the teachings of "Moon Teacher", and her Seminars. There is disillusionment on the part of some of those that paid to attend the seminar.

When the final numbers are examined it appears as though only 3 of the 23 participants experienced an Out of Body sensation. The other 20, including myself felt they were rooted in their chairs, reading the typing on the screen. I think that this requires further investigation on my part.

"Moon Teacher" comes into the room, and I ask ASL, which means Age, Sex, and Location. She hesitates, and then answers 42, Female, Houston Texas; I thank her for the information, and allow her into the room. Some of her Seminar participants, tell her quite straight forwardly they did not have an Out of Body experience. She begins to berate them, telling them they did not concentrate hard enough on the exercise like the ones that did have a good experience. She encourages them to try again the following week, when they will get a different exercise to work with. Some of the participants tell her they tried to copy the exercise, but the copy function would not work. "Of Course it wouldn't" she tells them. "It is copyrighted material, and I have adjusted the Settings so that it can't be copied." This angers some of the participants; I have to cut the conversation of at that point so that the atmosphere in the chat room won't disintegrate into chaos.

I appoint another moderator, and withdraw from the chat room. I take a small amount of smudge, smoke the directions, the room, and ask the helping Spirits to come, and take care of James body. Now I leave James body, rise up above the city, and go out into the Earths realm. I know where Houston Texas is, because I have referred to a map in the office, so I make my way to that city.

I am over the city of Houston, looking for the Spirit that is "Moon Teacher" I am led to a small house on the Southerly side of Houston, and there I find her sitting in front of the computer. She is a medium sized person, a bit older than the 42 years she told the room, but she is definitely female, easy to tell because she it totally naked. I enter her room, and look for some identifying oddities that I can describe to her later, and she will know that I have been there to see her.

I see a red mark under her right breast; it looks like a sleeping dog, and is about an inch long. There is a large dark blue bruise on the inside of her left thigh, in her hand she holds a red & yellow rod that looks like a male penis. She laughs at something on her computer screen, then inserts the rod into her female parts, and begins to push it slowly in, then out. I have seen enough, so I leave her, and rise up above the city.

My attention is drawn to a flickering light not far from "Moon Teachers" house, so I go over to have a closer look. It is a fire on the side of one of the huge white tanks that are being used to store gasoline. It occurs to me that I had better get back to James, and raise an alarm. I rush back to James, enter the body, and thank the helping Spirits for their care of James body.

I sign back into the chat room, and address "Moon Teacher". " You had better call the fire Department or who ever is in charge of the Gasoline storage tanks not far from your house, and tell them there is a fire on the side of one of the tanks" I tell her. "Your full of shit ZXN37, how could you possibly know anything about where I live?" I tell her I was just there, describe the red mark under her breast, the fact that she was naked, and had a large blue bruise on the inside of her left thigh. I didn't get to tell her about the red and yellow rod, because she immediately left the chat room.

One of the other participants of the room said OMG (Oh My God) CNN just flashed a news item on the screen, there has been a huge explosion on the south side of Houston, a large gasoline storage tank is on fire, and they are evacuating people from the homes within a 5 mile radius.

I remark that this is probably why "Moon Teacher" departed so quickly, everyone in the chat room agrees, and we leave it at that. Some have caught on to my telling "Moon Teacher" about her markings, and nakedness. "Can you leave your body ZXN37?" they ask. I tell them that under the right conditions, and at the time of Death every Spirit can leave the Earthly body.

One of the other moderators admonishes me; "We do not speak

of Religion in the room ZXN37." I am not speaking of Religion I am merely telling what is, besides Religion would not tell anyone that the Spirit can be free to leave the body. Every one agrees with me so the discussion about Spirits leaving the body continues. A participant gives me the address for the North American Shamanic Foundation, tells me that I would find the organization very interesting, and suggests that I contact the Foundation.

A Shamanic Adventure

I find the web page of the North American Shamanic Foundation, and begin reading their information, it is an organization dedicated to the preservation, and enhancement of Shamanism. There are Seminars held around North America to teach basic Shamanism. There is one in Everret Washington that will be held in 30 days, so I register for it and plan to attend.

Johanna assures me that she will manage the monitoring station while I am away, and Anne advises that her nephew in Vancouver will have 10 rolls of fencing for me to pick up on the way home. I will have to take the blue truck to carry that load. Once everything is planned, I read some of the Shamanic books so I won't be totally in the dark when I get to the Seminar.

Three days before the Seminar I put gas in the truck, and I am away headed west towards the mountains, and Everret Washington. The highway has 4 lanes, and the little truck hums along easily, off in the distance I can see mountains, which loom larger as I get closer to them. Very soon I am traveling through the mountains, the road is still good, but has dropped to 2 lanes. After traveling for some time I begin to feel sleepy, so I find a rest area along side the highway, and pull over. There is a mattress, and sleeping bag in the back of the truck, so I climb in, lock the door from the inside, then crawl into the sleeping bag, within moments I am fast asleep.

It is just getting light when I awake, and climb out of the back of the truck, there is a light rain falling, so I waste no time climbing into the cab. I start the engine, am about to pull away from the rest area when a young female steps in front of the truck. I stop, she comes to my side of the truck, I roll down the window, and she asks if I am going to Vancouver. "Yes I am going to Vancouver" I tell her. Then she asks if she can come with me, it is raining, she is soaking wet, I am going her way, so I tell her ok, she runs around to the passenger side, and gets in. I pull out of the rest area, and head towards Vancouver.

"A prick in a semi tried to get me into the bunk back there, and when I wouldn't go he kicked me out" she said. I assume she must have been out there in the rain for quite some time to get as wet as she seems to be. I turn on the heater so that the warm air will help her dry out a bit. Out of the corner of my eye I can see her wiggling out of her wet jeans, and make sure I keep my eyes firmly on the road. The next thing I see is her putting a white flimsy garment up on the dash where the heat comes out. I sneak a quick peek at her, and see that she has no clothes on from the waist down. "You can look if you want to" she says. "Does this seat go back", I tell her there is a little handle on the outside of the seat that makes it recline, she finds the handle, and I hear the seat being adjusted to the reclining position.

The gas gauge is showing empty when I reach a city called Kamloops, so I look for a gas station. I am about to pull into a station when I remember the girl in the passenger seat is naked from the waist down. I take my jacket, and cover her, then pull into the station.

I am busy filling the tank, when I see her get out of the truck, and go to the women's washroom. The shirt she is wearing barely covers her nakedness, and I hope that no one notices her as she walks to the washroom, and back to the truck. When I go to pay for the gas the attendant says, "Your daughter has a nice ass." I pay the bill, go to the washroom, and make a hurried return to the truck. As I pull away from the station, I tell her she could have put her jeans on when she got out of the truck, everyone there would not have seen she was naked.

"Did I piss you off?" she asks. I tell her no, but I am not used to having young naked girls flouncing around showing everyone their nakedness. I am a bit flustered, because I have not seen a naked female in a long time, except for the Moon Teacher, and that was not a pleasant experience.

Back on Sirius B, bodies are not made with male and female parts, due to the fact there is no need to expel any waste materials. In James's body I have learned to use his part for expelling waste water, but something in the memory banks seem to tell me that it can be used for something else too.

The rest of the trip to Vancouver was uneventful she reclined the seat, covered herself with my jacket, and slept most of the way. "Where are you going? She asked as we were coming into the city of Vancouver. I tell her that I will be making the turn to go to Everret Washington. There is a strip of motels on the side of the road, and she indicates that we should pull into the driveway of one. When we are parked in front of the office, she tells me to go in and register for a room for the night. "What for?" I ask. "Don't you want to fuck me?" she says. I am embarrassed to tell her I have no idea what she is talking about, so I say nothing, and go into the motel office. I fill out the register give the attendant $55.00 for the night take the keys for #32, and go back out to the truck. I give her the keys, watch her go into the room, then I get back in the truck, and drive out of the motel parking lot headed for the United States border.

Crossing the US border was very easy, and soon I am driving along a really well kept 4 lane divided highway. I keep looking for a rest area so I can pull in, and get some sleep. It occurs to me that I could have been sleeping in a nice bed at the motel, had I not bolted because I was embarrassed. I resolve to find out what this "fuck" is all about so the next time a female asks me, I will know what to do. Finally there is a rest stop at the side of the road, I pull the truck into a parking stall, get in the back, and in a short time I am fast asleep. The next thing I know it is light outside, and some one is pounding on the side of the truck. I unlock the door, climb out, and see that the person pounding on the truck is wearing a uniform; including one of the biggest pistols I ever remember seeing. The badge on his chest says "Washington Highway Patrol" so I am sure he is a Policeman.

"We don't like people sleeping in the Rest areas" he says. I tell him that I was under the impression that was what "Rest" meant. He explains there are many thieves, robbers, and other unsavory types that prey on people like me when they find them sleeping in the rest areas. I thank him for the information, get in the cab of the truck, and am once again on my way to Everret.

It is late in the afternoon when I reach the site where the Seminar is going to be held, I am just in time for registration. I fill out the forms, hand them to the person at the registration table, who hands me a single sheet of paper that has the schedule for the Seminar written on it. I ask about sleeping accommodations, and am told there are motels in Everret, or I can drive into Seattle to find accommodations there. The information given for the Seminar indicated there were accommodations at the site.

I don't want to seem unfriendly, so I leave, and drive into Everret.

There are no vacancies in any of the hotels, or motels in Everret, but I do find a nice restaurant that serves fresh Salmon. I have a good meal, then drive back to the site of the Seminar, pull into the parking lot, get out of the truck, and go for a walk around the grounds to familiarize myself with the location of the Seminar. I am able to locate two washrooms at the Seminar site. I return to the truck, crawl in the back, and go to sleep for the night.

The next morning I am up early, go to the washroom, wash myself, and prepare for the days activities. Some of the other participants arrive on the site, we exchange greetings, but they are very aloof, and do not carry a conversation on for long. The doors to the Seminar site are opened, we go inside, and are told to sign the attendance sheet. When it is my turn to sign I move to the table, and look at the sheet. It has a slot for "Name, Address, Degree/or Major study" I sign my name, and put the address in the proper slot, but I am at a loss to fill in the Degree/or Major study slot.

I note that the participants who have signed above me all have a degree in Anthropology, or have indicated that they are studying it. I leave the slot blank.

The Seminar room is Round with windows on all sides except for the east side. The instructor is about 40 years old, the literature says he has a PHD in Anthropology, and is a Master of Celtic Shamanism. Wow! I am about to learn something from a Master.

We are all assigned a space on the floor in a circle around the room. The instructor is in the center; he begins the session by telling us how the ancient Celtic people used poetry to express the way they used to contact the Spirit world. He tells us how he recites poetry, and beats a small drum to get into a space where he can journey, and meet Spirits.

He encourages us to write a short piece of poetry that expresses a desire to meet the Spirits, we are given a few minutes to think, and write the poetry then he indicates that we can begin to journey. He starts to beat a small drum.

"Don't we smudge the circle before Journeying?" I ask. The look I get from everyone in the room including the instructor, tells me that I should have kept my mouth shut. I am told rather curtly that smudging is something that other people who try and follow the Shaman way do, but the Celts never used the smudge. The instructor begins to beat the drum, and all recline on mats, to listen to the drum.

I find this non-smudging of the circle odd, because all of the books on Celtic Shamanism that I have red in James library, speak of smudging, and are very specific about how it is done. I say nothing more, and lay back on my mat. The drumming goes on for quite some time, when it stops all participants sit up, and listen as the instructor tells of his journey. Then everyone in the room is invited to tell of their journey. It seems all of the participants have traveled to marvelous places, and seen many good Spirits.

It is my turn to tell of my Journey I tell them I have drawn a blank, and I did not have a journey, or dream of any sort. The instructor berates me, saying that I have not concentrated hard enough on the poetry, and I need to practice more.

The morning session is over, and we are told to return early in the afternoon for the next session.

The participants' file out of the seminar room, I follow them as they make their way towards a large building beside the parking lot. Apparently lunch is being served in this building; a sign says "Entrance by Invitation only". I ask the person in front of me what that means, and he shows me a slip of paper that has the invitation to lunch written on it. I don't have a slip of paper so I leave the area and go to my truck.

It is soon time for the next session so I follow the participants back to the seminar area.

The instructor is engaged in a deep conversation with a young lady that had a particularly colorful journey in the morning session. Others join in the conversation, which takes quite a long time, finally the instructor breaks from the group, and calls for the attention of the participants. The instructor tells us we are going to make a journey to visit the fairies that live in the underworld, we will each find a fairy, and bring a message back to give to the group.

The instructor begins beating on the drum, and all participants including me lay back down on the mats. I am intrigued by the thought of visiting the fairy world, but I remember the First Rule, and remain in James body as the instructor beats the drum.

When the instructor stops beating the drum everyone sits up. The instructor tells of his journey, meeting the fairy king, and being told that many of the participants will go on to accomplish great deeds. Then the other participants start telling of their journey.

The young lady of the morning's session tells a magnificent story of seeing many fairies, and of participating in an exhilarating dance with male fairies both young and old.

My turn to tell of the journey comes, and once again I have to admit I have drawn a blank. The instructor again questions my attitude, saying that perhaps I should not have come to participate. I tell him the seminar was advertised as a beginner's seminar, which indicated that novices would be able to learn about Shamanism, and journeying.

The instructor tells me that perhaps if I had attended one or two classes in anthropology I would understand the way that people accessed the realm of other realities. It seems that there are Educational prerequisites that should be followed before one even considers learning about Shamanism. I have to admit to myself that I am not learning anything, and the trip has been a waste of time so far. That evening I am sitting in the truck when I see the instructor and the young lady with the colorful dreams going into a room at the large building.

I sleep in the back of the truck that night, and then attend the Seminar the next day. The morning session goes along the same way, except the instructor seems agitated, and the young lady stares off into space most of the time. During the morning Journey I again have no vision.

Before the afternoon session I dig out my smudge dish, and smudge my area, calling on the Spirits to protect James body. After some preliminary talk the instructor tells the participants to journey, to find a vision of what has occurred, and what will be for their journey.

I lay back on the mat as the instructor starts his drumming. Now I have a vivid picture of the instructor and the young lady, she is naked and he is kneeling between her spread legs. She has a tattoo of a snake on the inside of her right thigh; I can see her female parts' pulsing as the instructor comes ever closer to her.

The instructor is naked also, and his penis is dangling from his crotch. I see him playing with it, moving it up and down, but it still just hangs loosely, he trys to put it in her female parts but it bends and falls out.

The scene switches, and I see destruction all around me, the seminar meeting place has crumbled to the ground, and there is water flowing over the area. I can feel the shaking of the Earth, and realize that an earthquake had occurred very near to the site. A voice tells me that it is time to move away from the area.

The drumming stops, I return to James body, sit up, and listen to the participants tell of their journeys. When it is my turn the instructor call the name of the person next to me to tell their Journey. "What about mine?" I ask. "You don't Journey! The instructor says.

"Oh but this time I had a vision." I tell him. The instructor says, "It had better be good then, you have wasted a good amount of the seminar's time so far". I started by telling of the vision of the young ladies tattoo, and continued to tell what I had seen the instructor trying to do. The instructor was very red in the face, and shouted "That is enough, shut the fuck up!" I saw the young lady stand up then run from the room. Then I told of seeing the water, and the earthquake, when I finished I was aware that all of the participants were leaving the seminar room.

The instructor and I were left alone in the seminar room. "You ruined the seminar you son of a bitch." He said. I could not understand where he was coming from, as I was not the one trying to mount the young lady, and only told what I had seen in my vision. I told the instructor that he should learn to smudge maybe things would go better for him. I saw his energy turn bright red, and instantly knew I should leave the area. This was the first time I had seen some one's energy field turn to a different color so vividly.

I went to the truck, left the area, and drove north towards Vancouver. The events of the 2 days seminar swam round and round in my mind as I drove. I reached Vancouver, found Anne's nephew, loaded the fencing she wanted, and soon was on my way to Edmonton. I arrived in Edmonton 2 days later with no mishaps. On the way I heard a news report there had been a serious earthquake in the Seattle/Everret area, and parts of Everret were under water. I guess some visions are better than others, and I felt relieved that all the participants had left the area.

When I get to the monitoring station Johanna is there, waiting to hear all about the Seminar. I begin to tell her about the trip, when

I get to the wet young lady Johanna starts to laugh. I ask her what is so funny, and she tells me I had a perfect opportunity for sex, and turned it down. Oh is that what the young lady wanted, guess I was pretty naïve, just as well, after seeing the vision of the instructor trying to put his penis in the young lady of the seminar, I don't think I want to try that any time soon.

Lessons in Reality

I found a Drumming Circle listed in the Shamanic Foundation's directory, and enrolled in the program. When I get to my first session I find it is a large Gym of an elementary school. We have been told to bring our own mats, and sleeping bag, or some other kind of blanket. The leader of the group welcomes me, and assigns a space on the floor to be my area. I put my mat and sleeping bag down, sit and wait for further instruction. The people coming to this drumming circle are of all ages, and of both genders, but they are very much friendlier than the ones I met in Everret. We are arranged to form a circle on the Gym floor.

The instructor moves to the middle of the circle, begins by explaining that we will be journeying tonight to find our Spirit Animal, we are to lie back on our mats, listen to the drum, and feel our Spirits move to the Animal Spirit world below, where our Spirit Animal will meet us. The instructor has us stand quietly at the end of our mats while she smudges the circle, and asks for the Spirits to guide our journey. Then we are instructed to lie back on our mats while the drumming starts.

When the drumming starts I hear the instructor's voice instructing the participants to go deep down into the earth to a calm green area, then be aware of the animals, one of the animals will be very close to you, and you will feel its Spirit.

The Spirit animal will be our guide in the Spirit world, we are told to go with the Spirit animal, to visit the Spirit Animal world below. The drum keeps a steady rhythm, but I can't seem to get any kind of vision, I almost fall asleep, then the drumming stops, and we are told to return to full consciousness.

Just as the people did on the Everret Seminar, many of the participants had very vivid journeys, and met many beautiful Spirit Animals. One woman in particular was very descriptive of all she saw, the Spirit of the Deer, the wonderful flowers, and trees of the Animal Spirit world, she saw it all. Others told of seeing different animals, and scenery.

I was stymied once again, and had to tell the circle that I had no vision. The Circle was breaking up; all the participants were leaving when the instructor came over to my mat.

"Don't worry about not journeying," she told me. "Sometimes it is hard for a beginner to get in to the right frame of mind to see in to the other worlds." She encouraged me to keep trying, and come to the next session. I was looking forward to the next session, because I thought the visions they all talked about would come to me if I kept practicing.

A few days before the next session was to take place I received a phone call from the woman that had the vivid journey; she advised that the session would be cancelled, due to the unavailability of the school Gym. There was a large room in the upper part of my building, so I offered the use of it. My offer was accepted, the session was booked to the room on the following Sunday.

On the appointed day Johanna came in to run the monitoring station, while I went to meet the participants. They began to arrive, one of them told me the Instructor would not be able to make it to the session, and we probably would not have any smudging or drumming. I went down to my studio, got smudging supplies, and my portable tape recorder, with a Shamanic Journey tape.

There were 25 people in the room when I returned, I set up the tape recorder, and then began to smudge the room. One of the people told me I was doing it in a different way than the instructor always did. I told the group I was studying the Celtic way, and this is how I had been instructed in using the smudge.

This was a satisfactory answer, so I completed the smudging of the room, which included calling the Spirits of the Ancestors to assist in the journey. I turned on the tape recording, and layback to listen. I did not journey, but was able to see all of the others, and some were deeply into the trance created by the music on the tape.

When the music stopped the participants slowly sat up, some of them seemed really spaced out. They began telling their journeys, most were very colorful. When it came the woman who always had vivid journeys time to tell her journey, she began by describing an incredible room she had visited, the walls were light green, there was a stone circle on the floor of the room with a crystal growing out of a center stone. She saw a shelf on three sides of the room, with various stones and crystals on it. She saw a stick with tiny bells attached to it, and a small crystal mounted on the end. In the center of the circle above the stone with a crystal growing from it was a bench or table.

She became aware of Spirits in the room, and then could see them clearly, there were 28 of them, young, old, and in between. Two of the Spirits really stood apart from the rest; they were a huge man, and a lovely older woman. The Spirits came close to her, and told her she was welcome in the healing room, she could stay as long as she wanted, and come any time she needed to have help from the Spirits. Then her journey ended.

There were more journeys told; then a woman opposite the room from the woman with the vivid journey told us that she too had a similar journey, but she had not seen the details of the room as clearly. The Spirits were very interested in her presence, telling her they were helping Spirits, there to assist journyers in finding the answers to causes of distress that made people ill. She too saw the big Spirit, and the older woman, both spoke to her as they did to the first woman. They told her she would be welcome any time, and to come back soon. The journey ended.

When all the participants had shared their stories, I suggested that we go down stairs to the waiting room area, there were chairs there, and I would put tea on for the group. All accepted the invitation, and we went to the downstairs area. I went to the kitchen area, put a large pot of tea on to steep, and then I went back into the waiting room area.

My studio was adjacent to the waiting room, so I asked the first woman who had seen the green room if she would like to see my studio. She said she definitely would, so I unlocked the door so she could go into the studio. She did not go in! She stood in the doorway with her mouth hanging open, her face was frozen in a really weird position, and her eyes were big like a deer's when it is caught in the headlights of an oncoming vehicle. The room she was looking in to was the same room she had just described in minute detail from her vision, everything she had described was just as she said it was.

The other woman that had seen the Spirits came and stood behind the first woman. The second woman assumed the same demeanor as the first. One by one each of the participants came and looked into the room, some of them had written the journeys down, and compared their notes to see the details of the room.

I went back down to the kitchen to get the tea, when I returned none of the participants were there, they had all left. The studio door was open; there was no sign anyone had been there. I knew for sure neither of the women had ever seen my studio before, so they had gone there in their vision in order to describe it and the Spirits that came to help me when I was working with a client.

I took the tea, and went to the monitoring station. I told Johanna what had transpired with the circle, and how the women were in awe of having such a vivid real vision, but I couldn't explain why every one left so hurriedly. "REALITY" The word struck my mind like a hammer. "That is what got them." Johanna said.

"It is a lot of fun to go to these drumming circles, and imagine all sorts of nice things, and sweet animals to see, but when it becomes real like it did today the fun stops, and they can't handle it." I knew she was right, but I had not experienced it so vividly, I suppose that is what caused all the participants at the Everret Seminar to leave so quickly also.

The next week I tried to contact some of the drumming circle participants including the woman with the vivid journey. Most of their phones were no longer in service; I was able to speak to none of the participants. I finally contacted the Instructor; she advised me that the drumming circle had been disbanded; I would not be welcome at any further circles that she held. I tried to get a reason for the disbandment, and my exclusion from future circles, but the Instructor hung up. I tried phoning her again, but she would not answer.

A month later I received an invitation to attend a Seminar in Helena Montana. I made plans to attend, Johanna indicated that she would like to go with me, so I arranged for Garth to run the monitoring station, and told Johanna she was welcome to come with me.

Helena

The Seminar started on Friday afternoon at 3 pm with registrations, so Johanna and I started out on Thursday morning. We took turns driving, and arrived in Helena just after noon on Friday. I had reserved a double room at a Motel close to the Seminar site, so we registered, and went to the room to unpack our suitcases. Johanna lay down on the bed and was soon fast asleep; I got ready, and went off to register for the Seminar.

The participants at this seminar were very different from the ones that attended the Everret Seminar; they were down to earth people, very friendly, and quite open to striking up a conversation. I spent 3 hours meeting people, and discussing various techniques used for journeying. When I left the Seminar site I had the feeling this would be a very productive Seminar.

The next morning I eagerly went to the Seminar, which was being held at the University. I found several of the people that I met at the registration, in attendance with their mats spread out in a circle on the floor. I found a spot on the South side of the room that wasn't taken, and spread my mat out, and then I unpacked my smudge pot that I had brought with me, and took my wand out of its case.

The lady on my right side looked at the wand, and asked what it was. I explained to her that a Celtic Shaman always had a wand that helped him with his journey work, Mine was made up of a special dry branch that had fallen from an alder tree, then a seeing eye crystal was fitted in a small hole in the end of the branch, to complete the wand there was 9 silver bells attached with leather straps. When a Shaman was going to journey, the wand was shaken to ring the small bells; this was a signal to the Spirits the Shaman wished to visit their Realm.

We had been instructed to bring a stone the size of a grapefruit with us to the Seminar, I unpacked mine, and put it along side my mat. I noticed that all the others had done the same thing. The lady on my right showed me that she had her stone also.

The instructor that was conducting the Seminar was very different to the one that was at the Everret Seminar. He explained the method of journeying in detail, advising the Seminar that one should never try to journey unless the circle they were part of was properly smudged. He then proceeded to demonstrate the proper method of smudging. His method was exactly the same as mine except he did not call the helping Spirits for assistance. The instructor completed his smudging of the circle, and then asked one of the participants to give him her stone. We were instructed to partner up around the circle. I partnered with the lady to my right.

The instructor held the stone he had taken from the participant, held it in his left hand, and began to tell the participant her story according to the marks he saw on the stone. The participant had an astonished look on her face as the instructor told the story he saw on the stone. When the instructor finished with the story he told us that all stones carried the story of a Spirit. When we chose the stone that we brought with us to the seminar it was not random, but rather the stone had attracted our attention, because it was our stone, and held our story. There were many expressions of disbelief, but we were encouraged to read our partners stone.

I took my partners stone in my left hand just as the instructor had read the one he had read. I began to see pictures on my partner's stone, the name Helen was clearly spelled out on the one side of the stone, there was a figure under the name that appeared to be holding a instrument of some kind, and then there was a fuzzy picture that looked like a figure bending over a bed. I asked my partner if her name was Helen, and was she a nurse. There was an intense look of astonishment on her face, she confirmed that her name was Helen, and yes she was a nurse.

There were other markings on the stone that indicated Helen would be travelling with 2 smaller persons. There was another figure on the stone that seemed to be walking away from Helen, and the 2 smaller persons. As I turned the stone over in my hand I saw a long trail that led beside a row of mountains, and then ended at the bottom of a very large mountain. There was another figure of the nurse that seemed to show her dancing happily around a stand of trees.

I told Helen what I had seen as I looked at her stone, she sat on her mat facing me, and then a tear appeared in her eyes as I finished reading the stone. "How could you have known?" she asked. I told her I didn't know anything it was the stone that showed me the story I told her, then I showed her the markings on the stone. Helen was truly amazed! She told me that she was thinking of leaving her boyfriend, taking her 2 little girls, and moving to Alaska. She had been offered a good nursing job in Anchorage Alaska. The dancing figure seemed to tell her that she would be very happy there.

I handed her stone back to her, she held it in her left hand, and looked for the marking I had showed her, the markings were gone! Neither of us understood why the markings would disappear, so we called the instructor over and asked him. "The story on the stone is only told once, and then it vanishes, if you saw her story on the stone, you are very fortunate." He told us.

I gave Helen the stone that I had found to bring to the seminar. She took it in her left hand, and stared at it while she turned it over and over in her hand. "Its blank there is nothing on it." She said. The instructor came over, and took the stone from her. He held my stone in his left hand, and examined it. "Your right Helen, there is nothing on this stone." He said. The instructor called the attention of the group, and told them he had encountered a blank stone, which was a very rare occurrence that he had only come across once before.

"We have one too!" exclaimed another participant on the other side of the circle. The instructor went over to the participant, and took the stone she held. He examined the stone as he had done mine. There was nothing on that stone either. The instructor was amazed to have found 2 stones in this circle that had no marking on them.

We proceeded to the journeying part, and all the participants seemed to have good experiences. I had no particular reason to journey, so I lay on my mat, and just left my mind drift to the sound of the instructor's drum. I was able to see mountainous areas, with green grasses, and rivers flowing through meadow like surroundings.

The second day of the seminar we were told to journey to find the answer to a question that our partner asked. Helen asked me to see if she would be successful if she went to Alaska. I rang my shaman bells, lay back on my mat, and journeyed off to find Helen's answer as the instructor sounded his drum. The answer was that Helen would be indeed successful in Alaska, I saw her with a dark haired man, and her children, and they all seemed to be very happy. When the drumming stopped I told Helen what I had seen.

Across the circle the woman whose stone had no markings had been asked by her partner to journey, and find out is a deceased friend's father should be invited to his memorial service.

All talking ceased as the woman who had journeyed began speaking. "I went to the gathering place of the Spirits, and yes indeed I saw your friend as well as many others. Your friend told me that he was ok where he was, but he missed you and his friends on Earth. He said that his father would be really disappointed if he was not invited to the Memorial Service. Your friend also told me that you should not blame yourself for his passing, because it was his idea to initiate the sexual activity in the first place, his heart failed due to his not taking care of his health.

Your friend told me to tell you he would remember the strawberry birth mark on the inside of your right thigh until the end of time." "How could you have known!" her partner shouted.

There was a heavy rustling of feet, and gathering of mats, in less than a minute all of the participants and the instructor had left the seminar room. The woman who had told of her journey sat on her mat with a quizzical look on her face. I sat on my mat across from her, and wondered at what I had just witnessed. "What happened?" she asked. "REALITY" that was the only answer I could think of.

"Can I hold your wand?" she asked. For some reason I felt comfortable with her, and agreed to let her hold my wand. Her name was Irene; she came from Missoula Montana, and like James did not know who her father was. I questioned her further, and found out that she was her mother's first born child. (The mark of the Chosen One) We spent the rest of the afternoon comparing notes on our practices then parted to go to our homes.

Johanna and I drove back to Edmonton in a matter of 2 days, and I returned to the Monitoring Station to resume my mission.

A New Beginning

I had become a little frustrated at being shut inside the Monitoring Station for days on end without being able to see anything but the 4 gray walls. I began to work on drawing plans for a building that would house the Monitoring Station, and provide a studio so I could work at journeying. I designed a building 24' X 40' and was able to get approval for it to be placed on 2 lots that James had purchased in Tofield Alberta, which was 40 miles east of Edmonton.

In the summer of 1997 the little building was completed, we were able to move the Alarm Monitoring operation out to Tofield, and into the building. It was really great to have large windows on the side facing towards the street, and have the ability to see all of the traffic moving by road and rail.

The studio was windowless, it was set off at the rear of the building, and the only access to the studio was through a central waiting room that had an entrance door in the center of the building. When I first arranged the circle of stones that had been brought from the old studio, I smudged the directions, asked all of the Spirits to come to the circle, and asked the blessing of the ONE. This new studio took on all aspects of the old studio, felt really comfortable to be in, and had a very high Spiritual feeling.

It wasn't long before people were contacting Johanna and me to experience the healing that we practiced. One day Johanna came to the building with a dejected look on her face. When I asked her what was wrong she told me that we could no longer practice our healing, because the Province had passed a law saying that only Doctors could practice Alternative Healing.

Oh Oh! This was a development that I had not foreseen, after a quiet period of thought I began to wonder what the Government would have thought of Jesus's teaching, and healing.

I took the Bible and read some of the account of his time on Earth, there was a passage in the Bible that referred to Jesus as "Rabbi" the Holy teacher in the Jewish faith. It was clear the Government of the day during Jesus's stay on Earth wanted nothing to do with curtailing his teaching, and healing.

I searched the records, and information on the Internet, it appeared as if the Government wanted little to do with the affairs of a "Church". It followed that a Church could have internal procedures that allowed the leaders, or Ministers to lay their hands on members of the congregation for the purpose of Alternative Healing.

I searched the Internet, and found several sites that offered courses in the Ministry, Johanna enrolled in one of the courses, and I enrolled in a different one. It didn't take long for either of us to pass all the required exams, and soon we both held the title of Doctor of Divinity.

The next step I took was to register "The Gathering of the ONE Spiritualist Church" with the Government. We then organized a meeting of people interested in joining the Church. At the initial meeting of the congregation I presided over the ordination of Johanna as a Minister of the Church, while she did the same for me.

Once we had the Church in place, and we were ordained as Ministers of the Church, we began having people come to the studio to have us Balance their energies. This consisted of us laying our hands on their body, discerning the distribution of life energy in the body, and then re-distributing the energies so that the body was able to function normally. Both of us had many successful experiences with clients, and soon we had quite a few people wanting our attention. One of the prerequisites that people were required to sign on to was a membership in the congregation of "The Gathering of the ONE Spiritualist Church" before we would even talk to them.

About a month after we formed the Church, and began working with people, a gentleman came to the door; he presented his card which indicated he was an investigator with the College of Physicians, and Surgeons. He advised us that it was his job to investigate if we were indeed practicing Alternative Healing. I told him that we certainly were practicing Alternative Healing. He replied that we had better cease, and desist if we did not want to find ourselves in court charged with contravening the Law that said only Doctors could practice Alternative Healing.

I informed him that we were only performing internal procedures of our Church, and the only people we practiced on were members of the congregation. He said "Oh I see" then left. We have not had any more visitations since that time.

N D Es

Now that the question of hands on healing had been dealt with it was time to get back to the computer, and the mission. There were various news reports of many people experiencing Near Death Experiences, or NDE for short.

It was very interesting that so many NDEs were occurring in such a short time, this was evidence that the Collective had accelerated the program, and the time for the Earth's shift on its axis was drawing near.

I joined in several discussion groups that were attempting to find out what was going on to cause so many of these NDE reports. The media reported that 8.5 million people in the USA had reported a NDE in the past year, while the figure given for the European continent was 6.7 million.

There are many scholars that have pondered the NDE phenomenon trying to find the reason there have been such great numbers reported. They fail to understand that an advanced civilization would have the ability of transferring life energy or Soul from one body to another thereby allowing the Soul of an advanced being to influence the actions of the receiving body.

Many of those that were relating their experiences told of having changed the way they lived, acted towards their family, and other people around them. They could not explain why they behaved differently; it was as though the experience had cleansed their Soul.

I was able to pose a question to many of these people. "Is the Soul that occupies your body now, the same Soul that was present before your NDE?" Many people told me they were not sure, others simply didn't know, and a relatively small number did not even want to discuss the subject.

During the time I was involved with the Cherokee Eagles Nest Landing community one of the Legends that a North American Native group had told was that of the Rainbow Warriors who would come onto the Earth, be of all colors (Races), and would sleep until the end times. When the end time was at hand, the Rainbow Warriors would awaken, and guide the people to a new beginning.

Could it be somehow these people were given advance notice of the NDE transformations that were occurring at this very time in history, and is it possible that the ones who have experienced the NDE are in fact the Rainbow Warriors spoken of in the Legend? This would not be surprising given some of the information that Native American people had learned through their Vision Quests.

From my perspective that is exactly what is supposed to happen! This is what the Collective planned when they first started the switching of Souls. The ones who have experienced the NDEs will have their memories restored, and will be able to guide those around them in the WAY of the Collective. The people of Earth must come to understand the WAY of sharing with one another, looking out for one another, and of sharing unconditional love with all of the Universe

At the final rumblings of Earth just before it turns on its axis there will be great upheavals, and turmoil, many innocent bodies will perish, but those will be the fortunate ones, and their Souls will leave the realm of Earth to go to the ONE, and be part of the Collective. Those that remain alive will suffer great anguish. There will be wars fought over the remaining food supplies, and resources necessary in maintaining armed conflict.

Many will rush to their holy places, Churches, Synagogues, Mosques, and Temples, they will plead with their G.O.D.s to come and save them. There will be no great hand that comes from the heavens, to instantly curb the danger.

This is the time of the awakening of the NDEs, they must go amongst the people, and show them that all of Earth's people must join together in throwing out the mistaken beliefs that G.O.D.s will come to save them.

All those here on Earth are part of the ONE, and are here so that the ONE will know the experience of this time. The Soul that is part of the ONE can not be destroyed, only the Earthly bodies can be destroyed. The Souls that learn from the NDEs and follow the WAY will be taken to the home world to experience indestructible bodies, or have the choice to live again on a different planet to experience all.

Those who reject the WAY, and chose to live with aggression and malice toward others will be left here in the Realm of Earth as there is no place for that kind of Soul within the Collective.

The Family

One day I sat dozing in the warm afternoon sunshine that was streaming through the window that faced on to the street, someone knocked at the door of the waiting room. I went to see who the visitor was, when I opened the door I encountered a huge woman. She was at least 6'4" tall, heavily built, with long black hair, and dressed in what appeared to be animal skins. Pretty she was not, as a matter of fact one could only describe her as being ugly.

"I came to talk to you my brother." She said. "I don't think so" I replied as I searched James's memory banks for this person. "I have some pictures to show you my brother." She said as she pushed her way into the building, while brushing me aside.

We sat down at the table in the Monitoring Station, and she took some pictures out of an envelope she was carrying. She told me her name was Louise Roberta Bright Moon, and put the pictures on the table; sure enough there were pictures of James at a very early age, pictures that only could have been taken by someone at James's Grandmothers house. There were baby pictures, pictures taken of James around the farm with his aunts, all sorts of pictures. "Where did you get these, I have not seen them before." I told her. "My Daddy had them" she said. "He was your Daddy too."

No Way! James's mother had passed away years before without ever telling James the story of his conception, or who his father might have been, but I knew there was no way that this woman, and I had the same father. She reached in to the envelope, and withdrew another picture. This one showed James's mother with a dark skinned man. As I looked at the picture I went through James's memory banks I recognized the man as James's Uncle Giggs, who used to come to the farm where James grew up. He taught James to ride a horse, had given James a saddle, and many other things.

I told her that I knew who Giggs was, but I didn't think he could be my father; she turned the picture over, and showed me the date that was stamped on the back. August 1936! Hmm!! James was born in April of 1937, so that would make it about right, but I still thought it was impossible.

Giggs was a character to say the least, the reason everyone called him Giggs was because he wore blue chaps when he rode in rodeos. At the bottom of each chap there was a white circle with Giggs embroidered in the center. All the cowboys laughed at him because he couldn't spell right, the proper spelling was Jiggs, as in the comic Jiggs & Maggie.

I told Louise about going to the Ponoka Stampede with Giggs, and how the cowboys all laughed at him because he couldn't spell. She told me that he used to laugh at them because they didn't have a clue what it meant. When a man & woman engage in sexual relations our people say they are Gig a Gigging, and he was always Gig a Gigging, first he Gig a Gig my mom, then he Gig a Gig your mom, then he Gig a Gig John's mom, he Gig a Gigged 9 women, and fathered 11 kids, we are all half brothers and sisters. Wow! I had to sit for a while, and let this information filter into my brain.

"John saw you on the Internet my brother." Louise said "We know that you are the one that will see the 12th legend of our people to the end. Your Great Grandfather, who was known as "Moses who comes from the sky" gave the people an amulet, and told them when they found the person with those letters that are written on the amulet the 12th legend would be fulfilled, and the 13th legend could begin." She took a large amulet from her pocket, and laid it on the table. I could not imagine where it had come from, but the letters on the amulet were very clear, "ZXN". Once again I was totally speechless.

"Moses who comes from the sky also left us some machines that we have stored in a cave for all the years since he was with us. Your brother John was able to get one of them to move, and he thinks you are the one that will be able to get the largest one going.

He has taught your younger brothers to operate their own machines, so now Herman, Steven, and George all use the machines. We keep the machines out of sight, because John has told us of the satellites countries use to spy on one another, and it would not be good for one of the countries to see these machines." Louise smiled, as she told me about the machines.

I had a suspicion that the machines as they called them were vehicles from Sirius B, but I had no idea why James's Great Grandfather would have brought them to Earth, and left them with the family. The only explanation I could think of was these machines were to be used for the evacuation of Earth by humankind. I asked Louise what the 13th legend was about, she told me it said that the 112th chief of our people would lead the people away, and gave a time for the leaving.

Louise was the chief as she was telling me about the legend, but she was the 111th chief, and had not past the chief's mantle on. This would happen soon as she was not well, now that she had found ZXN she could rest easily knowing the people would be taken care of. Louise was going to return to the community later that afternoon, and asked me to go with her.

I called Johanna to come in and look after the Monitoring station, then agreed to go with Louise out to the community. I had no idea when I would get back, but when I explained to Johanna where I was going, she told me to stay as long as I wanted. Johanna could call on Garth or several part timers we had available.

The Community

Louise and I left the Monitoring Station; I was looking towards the street for a vehicle, but couldn't see one.   I asked Louise where her vehicle was, and she said John will be here any minute now, and then she walked towards an open field beside the Monitoring Station.

There was no sound, but a small machine about the size of a delivery van appeared in the field right in front of us. This machine came right out of a science fiction movie. It was shaped like every flying saucer ever depicted in movies, it was completely round, with a lower section that was about 30' across, and a smaller section 10' across on top. A door opened in the side of the top section, and a set of steps came up out of the lower section. Louise and I climbed the set of steps, and entered the vehicle. The interior of the vehicle was equipped with 4 seats for passengers, and a console on the one side that had 2 seats in front of it.

A man about my age sat at the console. "This is our brother John." Louise said. I shook his hand; he indicated that I should sit in the other seat in front of the console. Suddenly I was ZXN37 at home on Sirius B; I knew exactly what had to be done to operate this vehicle. John placed his hand on the console and the vehicle emitted as slight humming

---

sound as the inverter drive started. He moved the roller ball that was on the console in front of him, and we lifted away from the field.

The instruments on the console indicated an altitude of 450", and then the vehicle moved towards what I knew was west. The sides of the vehicle were translucent; we could clearly see where we were going, and everything around the vehicle. John kept the vehicle at the altitude of 450" heading in a westerly direction. I could see the Rocky Mountains coming ever so close as we moved along. John slowed our vehicle as we approached the foothills, and then we were descending into a large green valley. Once in the valley we moved directly towards the side of a mountain.

There was a large opening in the mountain, John put the little vehicle in to the opening, and once inside brought it to a stop.

We were inside a large cave that had been hollowed out of the side of the mountain. There were 3 other little vehicles the same size as the one we had come in, and another similar shaped vehicle that was much larger. John indicated the large vehicle, and said "That is the one that you have to operate my Brother we have tried to get it going, but none of us has the proper hand print. We think you are the one with the right hand print."

I recognized the larger vehicle as being a transport vehicle that was used for interstellar travel; it could carry many tons of minerals, or many passengers. This type of vehicle had both military and civilian capabilities. The 4 smaller vehicles were used for scouting, and exploration of planets. The larger vehicle had hatches on the side of the lower deck that opened, and allowed for the storage of the smaller vehicles.

I was curious about the origin of the larger vehicle, because I had been the G.O.D on one of them many lifetimes ago, and the memories of that time came flooding back when I saw this vehicle. I wanted to go onboard to have a closer look at the vehicle, but John insisted that we could do a thorough inspection of it the next day. The Family wanted to welcome me to their midst, and were waiting to begin the celebrations.

We walked to the opening of the cave, started down a path that led into a stand of trees, crossed over a bridge that spanned a small river, and then came to a large clearing on the valley floor. There was absolutely nothing in sight except for a few scattered bushes on the grassy plain. I asked John where the people and buildings were. He laughed, and said "You will see my brother." At that instant an opening appeared on the side of a small mound off to our right. John indicated that we should go into the opening. I stepped into the opening.

Unbelievable! That is the only way to describe the scene that lay before me inside the mound. There were rows of buildings shaped like the Quonset buildings one sees in the country side of Earth. These buildings were arranged in a circle around a much larger building that was in the centre of the development. There were people moving towards the larger building. "This is our community" John said. "We will go to the center lodge for the celebration"

We made our way to the large building, and joined with the other people who were going in to the building. All seemed very friendly, smiling, and waving at us. Once inside the building I saw a crowd that must have numbered in the hundreds. Most of the people were seated at tables that encircled a large round table in the centre of the building. This table was much different than circular tables used by most Earth people, because those sitting at the table were on the inside of the circle facing out towards the crowd.

John led me to the centre table, through the opening that allowed access to the inner circle. As I stepped through the opening I immediately recognized Sister Louise who had come to see me that afternoon. Louise was dressed in a magnificent white garment that hung from her shoulders, and reached almost to the floor. The garment was covered with many embroidered symbols, some of which I recognized from Sirius B. She wore a crown made of a similar material that her dress was made of. On the crown there appeared to be many shiny stones around the outer circumference.

Louise motioned that I should come over to her. I noted there were 11 chairs on the inside of the table facing the crowd, every chair except for 3 were occupied. "You will sit here on my right my brother." She said and indicated the middle chair of the 3. "Now I will introduce our brothers and sisters we are seated according to our ages, I am the oldest, you are next to me"

I saw that John had taken the empty seat to my right. Louise continued with the introductions; "This is John who you met this afternoon, next is Sister Rose, then Elena, Herman, Mary, Elizabeth, Steve, Mabel, and finally the youngest George, we all had the same daddy, this is your family Robert Louis." I started to correct her, to tell her my Earth name was James. There was no need! "I know you are called James by those around you my brother, but here we are known by the names our family gave us when we were born, so you are Robert Louis, just as I am Louise Roberta," she said with a finality that told me there was no use arguing the point.

We moved to our chairs, and sat facing the crowd. I had the distinct feeling that something was moving, and then discovered that our table was slowly rotating to the right. This allowed all of the people in the building to see those seated at the inner table. I would later learn this was also the council table, which was used to conduct the family's business.

Young men and women appeared bearing trays of steaming food, and began to serve all of the people in the building. They had platters of meat that they portioned out, but the centre table was being served from different platters than the crowd. The centre table was being served thick strips of what appeared to be semi-cooked liver. There was also a brownish vegetable, garnished with smaller green vegetables. I tasted a piece of the meat. It did not taste like any liver I remembered, but had a slightly salty sweet taste, and was so tender it chewed like jelly.

"You are eating the heart of a mighty Wapiti. Only our family will be served this delicacy at this meal. This is a great honor to celebrate the finding of ZXN, and the ending of the 12th legend." Louise said. "The vegetable is Bear root, covered with wild peas. The rest of our people are eating the meat taken from the Wapiti, so we all share from the hunt."

The meal was finished, and the tables cleared very quickly. There was complete silence in the building as an air of expectancy seemed to envelop the crowd. After a few minutes there was a rustling from the one side of the building as the young men and women who had served the meal came and took their seats.

At last Louise left her seat, and stepped to the inside middle of the centre table. She appeared to be standing on a smaller table. This small table rose out of the floor, and carried Louise up to a height where all of the people could see her above those seated at the inner table. We all turned our chairs so we could face her.

Louise addressed the people;

"My People this is truly a glorious day for our family, many times ago a Grandfather came to us, and we called him Moses who comes from the Sky. This Grandfather taught us many things about how we should live our lives, and treat one another. He gave us rules to follow, and then showed us how to make many wonderful things.

Many of the Grandfathers teachings are evident here tonight in the buildings of our community, and the bountiful life we lead. Grandfather told us before he went to be with the Great Spirit our world would not survive forever. He left us the machines in the cave of the future. Grandfather told us to always protect these machines from the eyes of those who live on the outside of our world. He also told us in the 12th legend that 5 brothers would be born to the family, and these men would have the ability of operating the machines. 4 of these brothers would be able to operate the smaller machines, and move at will around the Earth.

The large machine could only be operated by the fifth brother, because he had the experience of operating it before. Grandfather gave us an amulet with the sign of the fifth brother embedded in it. The 12th legend told us that the 111th chief of our family would find the fifth brother, who would be known in the world by the sign on the amulet.

The sign on the amulet I hold in my hand is ZXN, and today I the 111th chief of our family journeyed with my brother John to find the fifth brother.

I am very happy to tell you that I have found my brother Robert Louis, who is known all over the Earth as ZXN37. He is my fifth brother, and also the brother of all of the men and women seated at the inner table. There are 11 of us all together, we all had the same daddy, but not all had the same mothers.

Tomorrow we will take ZXN to the large machine to have him operate it. After we have confirmed that he is truly the fifth brother as spoken of by the Grandfather, I will have completed my mission as Chief. I will then pass the Chief's authority to my Granddaughter Roberta Louise so she can guide you through the 13th legend.

I have been your Chief for the past many years, and have always enjoyed the life we have had together. Now that I have completed the 12th legend it is my time to rest, and go to the Great Spirit. I will be waiting to greet you as you all come to join the Great Spirit. I Love you all!

The applause was thunderous! Everyone in the building was standing, and cheering, many had tears running down their face. Louise went to each of her siblings, and gathered them up in her arms one by one in a joyous hug. Then Louise went out amongst the crowd, and was greeted joyously by all those present.

The rest of us brothers and sisters spent the rest of the evening getting to know one another, they all wanted to know all of the details about my life, and experiences.

We talked and visited late into the evening until finally some of them were nodding off to sleep, and it was time to go to our sleeping rooms.

Venerable

My brothers and I left the gathering house, and made our way to one of the smaller buildings. We entered the building through an air lock that had a door towards the outside, a short corridor, and then another door that opened in to the interior of the building. The air inside the building smelled fresh and clean, almost like being in an Earth hospital. There were capsules along the sides of the building; some were open, while others were closed. I was shown to one of the capsules that was open.

"This is your sleeping area Robert, you will find everything you need for bathing, and dental cleaning on one of the shelves, put your valuables in the locking bin, and take the key. There are sleeping robes on the shelf, put your clothes in the bin at the end of the capsule. The washrooms are just behind your capsule, have a good sleep." John said then retired to his capsule.

I entered the capsule, it closed behind me, and I was alone in what appeared to be a very sterile environment. There were little signs that indicated what all the switches were for, lights, heat, cool, and lid switch to open the capsule. I found the toothbrush, toothpaste, and towels then went to the washroom, and got ready to sleep. I found the sleeping robes put them on, and deposited my clothes in the bin as John had instructed. When I lay down on the sleeping mat it felt as if I was floating in a soft bed of pillows.

I must have slept pretty soundly, because the next thing I realized was a voice saying, "Time to wake up Robert." I opened my eyes to see the interior of the capsule just as it had been when I first entered it. I moved to the end of the bed to get my clothes out of the bin. My clothes were gone! "Your garments are in the locker Robert." That voice again.

There was a locker beside the head of the bed. I opened the door, and there were clothes hanging inside, but they weren't mine. I took them out and lay them on the bed.

There was a pair of what appeared to be trousers, a long shirt like garment, and 2 pieces of underwear. I put the underwear on, and found the fit to be very good. There was a pair of undershorts, and a pull over shirt that was very snug fitting. I took the trousers, and slid my legs into them. The trousers were very tight fitting; the ends of the legs had a stocking like garment with a solid tread on the bottom.

Once I had the trousers on, I took the long shirt, and pulled it over my head. The long shirt fit well, it extended to just above my knees, and had tight cuffs at each of my wrists. For better or worse I was dressed, so I flipped the switch to open the capsule.

My brothers were standing by the capsule; all of them were dressed exactly as I was.

"It's time for breakfast Robert." George said. He led the way as we exited our building, and walked towards the centre building. The interior of the building had been transformed from the seating arrangement of the previous evening to one that had numerous tables arranged in neat rows. At the one end of the building there appeared to be a cafeteria counter. People were moving along the counter filling plates with food, then going to a table to eat. I joined the line, took a plate and filled it with what appeared to be scrambled eggs. I followed my brothers to a table, and sat down to eat. This was not scrambled eggs! The taste was like a pumpkin, or squash, but the texture was that of light fluffy eggs. I would later learn this food was from a large squash like vegetable the cooks had learned to cook in this fluffy manner.

After breakfast we went to the Cave of the Future, I was very anxious to examine the larger vehicle. I walked around the exterior of the vehicle; there was no indication of where one might enter. I could see the outline of the hatches where the 4 smaller craft would be housed, but that was it there was no similar outlines to show other hatches or entrance points.

I asked John how they had been able to remove the other smaller vehicles. John told me. "One day I was examining the big one, and moving around the outside of it. I saw what looked to be the outline of a hand on the edge of the vehicle. I put my hand on the outline, and holy! The hatch opened. I could see the smaller one inside. I got our brothers and we managed to slide the small one out of the hatch. I knew what the hand outline meant so I looked for it on the small vehicle, and sure enough there it was. I put my hand on the outline, a set of steps appeared, and a door opened at the top of the steps. I climbed the steps, and found myself inside the vehicle we came in yesterday. I looked for the hand outline, when I found it and put my hand on it the power came on, and the vehicle came to life. I spent a long time learning how to get the vehicle to move, but now I can go anywhere I want with it."

Of Course! I should have known "Biometrics" the vehicles would only operate if the proper hand it was programmed to recognize was placed on the terminal. We began to examine the large vehicle more closely looking for the terminal. One of the brothers shouted. "I've found it!" We all crowded around the outline he had found at the edge of the large vehicle. It was my turn. If the legend was to come true, the vehicle would come to life when I placed my hand on the outline.

One of the brothers suggested we should get Louise and our sisters to be there when I placed my hand on the outline so they could see for themselves whether the legend was true or not. George went running to get our sisters, while the rest of us milled around the vehicle enjoying the anticipation of something really awesome about to happen.

George came back with the women following not far behind him. I showed them the hand outline, and got Louise to stand beside me. This was her day as much as anyone else. When everyone was gathered around us I slowly placed my left hand on the outline.

There was a soft whirring that came from somewhere inside the vehicle.

A set of steps emerged from the leading edge of the craft, and unfolded till they reached the cave floor. At the same time another set of steps appeared on the upper side of the vehicles lower level. The second set of steps led to a door in the side of the upper lever, which was slowly opening. We all stood in awe, this vehicle had rested in this cave for many years, but now it had come to life as soon as I put my hand on the terminal.

They all followed me as I climbed the steps leading to the door in the upper level. We reached the doorway, and stepped into the interior. It was absolutely amazing! The floor of the room we were looking at had tables and chairs arranged in exactly the same configuration as the large building was the previous evening. There was even a small centre stage that we instantly knew would rise as the speaker rose to address those gathered in the room. The capacity of the room must have been in the thousands, which didn't seem possible given the size of the vehicle.

There was a sign over the entrance door which had one word on it. "Venerable" I knew that name, far back in ZXN37's memory the craft named Venerable was found.

This was the craft I had been G.O.D. to so long ago, but I had been of the impression Venerable had been lost on another world after I left it. How could it have gotten to Earth, and into this cave? If we found the memory banks of the craft I might know the answer.

I moved with out hesitation to a door on the opposite side of the room. The door opened to reveal a command centre built into the outer wall of the room. I moved over to the command console, there were 3 chairs facing the console. I sat down in the centre chair, and examined the console immediately in front of me. The instruments were a lot like the ones in the small ship that John operated, but there were a lot more of them.

There was also a hand outline on the left side of the console in front of me, there was a roller ball mounted where my right hand would touch the console. Between the hand points there was an unfamiliar looking keyboard that had keys with strange looking symbols on them.

The console in front of the chair to my right was laid out in a similar manner; there was a hand outline in front of the right chair also. The console on the left had no hand outline or roller ball, but did have the keyboard. Instinctively I knew that the left chair belonged to the Navigator, (NAV) it was this crew's responsibility to set the course to the crafts destination. The crew on the right was second in command, and responsible for the security of the craft.

There was a set of pedals on the floor in front of the centre chair, and the right chair. I knew immediately these were the manual override levers to vary the strength of the travel magnetic drive, to either decrease, or increase the speed of approach to any planet.

Louise and the family were standing behind my chair. It was time to see if the legend would be completed on this day. I placed my left hand on the hand outline, there was a soft whirring, a screen slowly rose from the console in front of me, and the wall of the craft in front of us slowly turned translucent. We could now see what was in front of the craft. There was a movement at the cave's entrance; it appeared as though a curtain was being lifted to allow Venerable to move out of the cave. I did not want to attempt moving the craft at that moment; I wanted to refresh my memory of how to operate it.

The screen on the console was much like those used on Earth as monitors on the computers, except the icons were not the same. The Message on the screen read "Welcome ZXN37." A dial on the keyboard moved a cursor on the screen; this was older technology that had been in use on Sirius B some time ago. Modern technology only required that one thought of what they wished to occur on the screen, and it immediately happened.

I moved the dial so that the cursor was over one of the icons, and pushed it down like one would click a mouse.

The screen changed and began displaying lines of information, which appeared to be a record of the craft's travels from the time it was constructed. "What does it say?" Louise asked. For the first time since I came to Earth, and took over to be the Spirit in James body I realized that the people of Earth were not able to understand the language of the Collective. When I entered James's body I inherited all of his capabilities, and was able to understand his language, the Collective must have to translate all of the information they give the Earth people.

I read some of the craft's log to the family, and they were satisfied that I knew what I was reading. This was a glorious day for them, for they had just witnessed the 12th legend of the family being ended, and was now ready to begin working towards the completion of the 13th legend. I placed my left hand on the hand outline for the second time, and Venerable began to shut down, the curtain closed on the cave entrance, the walls became solid, and the screen retracted into the console.

We made our way to the exit door of Venerable, climbed down the steps to the cave floor, and stood admiring the craft that we someday would board for a very exiting journey. I placed my hand on the outline, the door on the second level closed, and the steps retracted in to the surface of the craft.

Changeover

Later that day everyone gathered in the center building, the table configuration was assembled as it was the previous evening with all the tables encircling the center table. My brothers and I were ushered to a table at the front, and sat facing the center table. There were 13 women seated on the inner side of the center table. John told me that these were the 12 Council members and Louise who was the chief.

When everyone had entered the meeting room Louise stepped on the small table at the center, and slowly rose so that all in the room could see her.

She began to address all of those assembled.

"My Family! Today has been a wondrous day, for today my brother Robert Louis, or ZXN37 as he is known to the Universe, was able to operate the largest vehicle in the Cave of the Future. This means that all who are here at the end of the 13th legend will be able to board that vehicle, and leave this planet. It also means that I have completed all of the tasks of the 12th legend, and can at last rest, and go to the Great Spirit."

"The 13th legend tells us that in the coming days there will be much turmoil on the Earth's surface, and many people will perish. There will be many people who survive the upheaval; these people will be looking for a place where they can be safe.

This will lead to a great influx of people to the lands near our valley. It will be our mission to save as many of these people as we possibly can, which we will willingly do so long as they will agree to live with us in harmony, and Love. Those who are not willing to live this way will not be brought to our valley. At the appointed time the 112th Chief of our people will lead everyone in our valley to the great ship in the Cave of the Future."

"My Brother Robert Louis, ZXN37, will move the great ship out of the cave, and out into the Universe. This will be the final exodus of our people from the planet.

Then the planet will rotate on its axis, and all the surface of the Earth will be changed forever, all life that remained on the surface will be destroyed in an instance."

"Now I will call upon my Granddaughter Roberta Louise to come up to this stage, and join me."

A young woman approached the centre table, entered to the inner part then stepped up to the center stage to join Louise.

She was built much like Louise, same height, same wide shoulders, but was much more pleasant looking.

Louise put her hand on the young woman's shoulder, and said;

"This is my first Granddaughter Roberta Louise. The custom in our family is that the Chief hands the leadership of the family, over to her Granddaughter when her mission is completed. Today I have seen the 12th legend, and my mission as Chief fulfilled. I will now pass the Chief's mantle to Roberta Louise. She will be our 112th Chief, and complete the 13th legend."

Louise removed the headband and gently placed it on Roberta's head. She kissed Roberta on both cheeks, and then stepped from the centre stage. The people spontaneously broke into loud cheers, and thunderous applause.

Roberta stood quietly listening to the cheers and applause for her Grandmother. When the applause started to fade Roberta addressed the people.

"My Family! I am honored that my Grandmother has chosen me to be the 112th Chief. It will be my sacred mission to see the 13th legend through to the end.

I will count on the advice of the Council. I will also rely on my 5 Great Uncles to help me in completing the 13th legend. I also will lean on many members of our Family to give me guidance from time to time. I will do the very best I can to maintain our way of life, and the treasures we have. All of this I promise to you my Family."

Roberta left the stage, and made her way around the Council table, stopping at each chair to acknowledge each of the Council members. She walked over to her Grandmother and took the older Woman's arm. Arm and Arm the two women walked slowly out of the table, and slowly proceeded towards the main exit doors of the gathering lodge. The people once again applauded for as long as the women were in the lodge.

My brothers and I left the gathering lodge, and went to our sleeping quarters. We were about to move to our separate capsules when a young boy came into the sleeping quarters.

The boy told us that we should follow him to the Chief's lodge.

We went with the boy across the field to a large lodge set apart from the other lodges.

The Chiefs sign was above the door of the lodge, sister Elena was standing by the door. She motioned for us to follow her, turned and entered the lodge. We were a bit hesitant to follow because it was not the custom for men to visit the women's lodges. Elena again motioned that we should follow her, so that is what we did.

All of our sisters were in the center of the lodge. They were gathered around a bed on which Louise lay. Most of the sisters had been or were crying. "Come over here my brothers." Louise said. Her voice sounded very weak, certainly not the strong authoritive tone of voice we were all accustomed to.

We gathered at the head of Louise's bed, she looked very frail, and was apparently having some difficulty breathing. It was hard to imagine this was the woman that had left the gathering lodge not so very long ago.

"It is my time to go to the Great Spirit my brothers, I have been very ill for awhile, but now my mission is completed, I can finally let go. I want Robert Louis to go with Mary Two Owls when she puts my bones in the Cave. I want you to know the ceremony my brother so that you may assist Mary until it is her time, and then you will be able to do the ceremony for others who's Spirit has left to be with the Great Spirit."

"My brothers I ask you all, Robert, John, Herman, Steven, and George to do all you can to see that our Family is safe from harm.

As my passing wish I want you all to help Roberta as she faces the challenges of leading the Family in the coming turbulent days." In unison we all said. "Yes Louise we promise to do as you wish, and keep the Family safe from harm." One by one we bent and kissed our sister Louise on her forehead.

Our sisters followed suit, and filed by the head of Louise's bed, bent and kissed her gently on the forehead. We all formed a circle around Louise, holding hands we began to move in a circle around the bed. Suddenly one of the sisters gasped. I looked at Louise, and saw what appeared to be a light bluish gold cloud rising from her body. Our sister Louise's Spirit left her body, and was gone from all of us.

It took a while for the realization to sink in to all of the sisters, and brothers. Finally after a long period of silence sister Rose broke the circle, and told us the women were coming to get Louise's remains, and prepare her for the Cave of Bones.

None of us had anything to say as we returned to our sleeping lodge. The other brothers had known Louise much longer than I had, and they were feeling a heavy loss. I had not known her for very long, but I too felt a heavy sadness as I entered my sleeping capsule. I prepared my self and crawled into my bed. I did not fall asleep for a long time, because I was thinking about all that I had learned in the past days, and what I was to learn about the Cave of Bones.

Cave of Bones

"It is time to wake up ZXN37" There was that not so friendly voice again. Very reluctantly I sat up on my bed, and slung my legs over the side. I went to the locker to get my clothes for the day. What a surprise! The uniform that I had worn the day before was not there. In its place there was a selection of white skin garments. There was a long piece of skin on one hanger, a pair of leggings on another hanger, and a long beaded shirt on still another hanger. On the floor of the locker there was a pair of moccasins made out of the same white skin. The moccasins were beaded with many of the same patterns that were on the shirt.

I was wondering how all of these garments were supposed to be worn, when someone knocked on the capsule. It was John.

"We are waiting for you." He said. I told John I was trying to figure out how to put the garments on. He took the leggings from the locker, held them up so that I could step into them, and then had me hold them up while he got the long piece of skin, which he placed between my legs. There were tie rope on the front and rear of the leggings that John tied under the long skin at the front, and back. I later learned the long skin was called a loin cloth. I pulled the shirt over my head, and stepped into the moccasins. We were ready for the day's activities.

Mary Two Owls joined us for the morning meal; she was dressed in a long dress with beaded patterns on it that were similar to the ones on my shirt. Mary told us the story of how the ceremony that she and I were about to do had its origin.

The first woman of our family found the cave on one her walks to explore the valley. It was a large cave, and over the years the wind and water had carved out benches, or shelves in the side of the cave. When her man died, she prepared his bones, and placed them on one of the shelves at the rear of the cave.

When she felt it was her turn to go to the Spirit world she told her Granddaughter that she would make her the Chief, and then taught her the method of preparing the bones. Her bones were laid next to those of her man. That method, and the ceremony of laying the bones on a shelf next to the last one that was placed there has been carried through to this very day.

We finished our meal, Mary Two Owls told me to follow her as she made her way towards one of the lodges on the outer edge of the community. We entered the lodge. I was not prepared for what I saw! There was a table covered with animal skins in the center of the lodge, a skeleton complete with its skull was lying on the table. The skeleton was shinny white, as if it had been polished. There were 2 containers on the floor at the foot of the table.

"This is your sister Louise's bones; the containers hold her flesh, and fluids." "The elder women of the community have prepared the bones of people who have gone to the Great Spirit since the first woman taught her Granddaughter. Everyone who passes to the Great Spirit in our community is prepared in exactly the same way. The fluids are drained from the body, and then the flesh is removed completely. The bones are then cleaned with a mixture of ashes, and the yellow powder from the stream."

"Once the bones have been prepared the kihcihtwawisiw makes the ceremony, takes the bones to the Cave of Bones, and gives the flesh to the wolves." Mary Two Owls Explained.

There was a circle of Stones around the table, and over to one side

I found a smaller table with smudging supplies on it. I prepared the smudge as I had learned to do then smudged the circle. When I came to the center of the circle, and the table on which Louise's bones rested Mary Two Owls joined me, we called for the Spirits of the Ancestors to come, and watch over the bones as we took them to the Cave of Bones.

Mary brought a stretcher like apparatus to the side of the table, we slid Louise's bones onto it. There were straps at either end of the apparatus that Mary showed me how to fasten around my neck, once the straps were in place I was easily able to support the apparatus with the bones on it. Mary picked up the 2 containers, and led the way out of the lodge.

All of the people of the community were lined up outside of the lodge, there was a corridor down the middle of the line up that Mary entered. I followed Mary carrying the bones of my sister Louise. As we walked along the corridor of people there was singing, a slow drum beat, and some crying.

There was an appaloosa horse hitched to a small wagon at the end of the line of people. Mary indicated that I should put Louise's bones on the wagon then placed the containers on the wagon in the receptacles that were made for them.

The horse seemed to know where we were going, because it started off heading across the valley with no urging. Mary and I fell in behind, and followed the wagon. We travelled for about 3 hours until the side of a mountain seemed to block our path. The horse veered to the right then entered a path at the base of the mountain, the path led up the side of the mountain. We travelled the path for almost an hour, and then I spied the entrance to a cave. This was The Cave of Bones.

The horse stopped at the mouth of the cave, I took up the straps on the stretcher, and lifted Louise off the wagon. Mary led the way and we stepped into the cave. The interior of the cave was well lit by some source of natural light; I could see the shelves along the side of the cave. There must have been 10 shelves at least 200 feet long. There was one completely bare, and another that was only about 1/3 covered. Mary led the way up to the one that was partially covered. She went to the last set of bones on the shelf, and indicated we should put Louise's bones next to that set. I put the stretcher on the shelf, and then very slowly pulled it out from under Louise's bones until at last they rested on the shelf beside the last set of bones.

We smudged the shelf, and bones thanking the Spirits of the Ancestors for watching over the bones, thanking the Spirits of the Cave for accepting Louise's bones.

"You will put my bones on this shelf soon ZXN37" Mary said. "Come I will show you the bones of our first ancestor."

She led the way to what was obviously the first shelf, and there right at the very first end was a perfectly preserved set of bones.

Next to the first set was a set of larger bones. This was the first couple that discovered the valley so many years passed. She was the 1st chief, and he was her man. We are all descended from this couple.

We stood for a moment of reverence savoring the knowledge that not many people could ever stand, and see the bones of their ancestors. Then Mary led the way back to the entrance of the cave.

Once outside the cave Mary took the 2 containers, and emptied their contents in to depressions in the stone to the right of the cave entrance. "We do this so that the wolves can come, and consume the flesh, then they do not bother the bones in the cave." Mary said. "No one from the community will ever come to this cave ZXN37, you will have to remember all of the ceremony, and do it by yourself. There is much crazy superstition about the bones walking around the cave, and sometimes the wind will blow out through the cave entrance making a mournful sound. This makes the people very afraid of going near the cave."

We rode on the small wagon as the horse pulled it back to the community. When we got back I went to my capsule, and took off the ceremonial clothes. My ordinary clothes from the day before were there in my locker, and I put them on. It was almost time for the evening meal. What a day I had experienced.

Back to Work

The following day I am awakened by that not so friendly voice in my capsule. "Time to wake up ZXN37" I got off the sleeping tablet and opened the locker to get my clothes, and to my surprise the clothes that I had worn in coming to the community were hanging in the locker. The clothes had been washed, and ironed, there was a pleasant clean odor coming from them. I got dressed, opened the capsule, and went looking for John.

John came out of his capsule and we headed over to the main lodge to eat our breakfast. I had many questions about the community that I wanted to ask John.

While we were eating I asked John about the visibility of the community, and why it was that as we approached it from the air it did not appear to be in the valley, there was only open land with a few trees scattered randomly around.

"Holographic shielding!" he said, and then went on to explain how he had learned to use the instruments in the shuttle craft to create a shield over the valley so that it appeared uninhabited. The shielding was translucent from below so the members of the community were not bothered by it. The Holograph duplicated a portion of the valley where people rarely went so that in the winter when snow was on the ground the shield showed a snow covered landscape when viewed from above.

The Cave of the Future also had a holographic shield that our Great Grandfather had put in place. Anyone looking at the side of the mountain where the cave was would only see the wall of the mountain with no opening in it.

We finished our meal, and walked out of the community to go to the cave where the craft were stored. John showed me the hologram projectors he had found in the craft, and had placed at strategic locations around the valley. It was these projectors that created the holographic shield over the valley.

There was other equipment in the cargo bays of the craft, but the brothers had not discovered how to use all of the equipment. John reasoned that Venerable must also have a cargo bay with supplies or equipment stored in it. We walked around Venerable looking for another storage area. I thought I remembered a hatch on the side of the ship by the entry stairs so we were very meticulous in examining that area.

John looked at the underside of the craft adjacent to the hand outline I had used to gain access to the craft. He found two hand outlines side by side. John tried using both of his hands on the outline with no success. Finally he suggested we put our left hands on the outlines according to the seating at the control centre. I placed my left hand on the left hand outline, and John placed his left hand on the right hand outline.

A soft whirring sound came from the craft, a door to the right of us started to open. This door was about 30 feet across, and was moving down to the surface of the cave. There was clicking sounds coming from around the craft, when we looked to see what was making the sounds, we discovered portholes in the leading edge of the craft. Something told me that we had just initiated the defense mechanisms that were built in to the craft.

The door reached the surface of the cave and locked into place with a heavy thud. We approached the opening, and looked to see what might be inside. It appeared to be a large cargo area that encircled an area at the centre of the ship. We went inside the cargo bay to see what other surprises might be in store for us.

We walked around the exterior of the bay, and discovered quite a few smaller doors that led to individual storage areas at the side of the cargo bay. One of these doors had a sign that read "Armory" over it, there was a hand outline beside the door. John placed his hand on the outline and the door swung inward with a soft whir. We entered the area and found we were standing in a large room with walls lined with hand held, and shoulder weapons.

The weapons were unlike any either of us had ever seen on earth. Both the hand held, and the shoulder weapons appeared to be light emitting devices. We decided to leave the weapons where they were, and close the Armory until we could learn the proper use of these weapons.

We found other doors along the exterior of the cargo bay, most contained supplies to support troops, uniforms, boots, rations, and toiletry items. There was also a storage area that held repair parts for Venerable its self. We found what appeared to be an elevator attached to the centre column of the craft.

Before entering the elevator we went to the side of the cargo bay door to see if we could find a way to close the door from the inside. There was a double hand out line on the wall beside the door. We placed our left hands on the outlines as we had done on the exterior, and the cargo bay door started to close.

We walked to the elevator, the door opened when we stepped in front of it, just like in the shopping centre doors did when customers walked in front of them. We entered the elevator, the doors closed, and the elevator moved upwards. When it stopped we walked out of the elevator, and to our surprise we were standing at the rear of the command centre.

We moved over to the control console, I took the centre seat, and John sat in the right seat. John placed his left hand on the outline in front of him, nothing happened. I placed my left hand on the outline in front of me, and the craft started to come alive the inverters started, the screen rose from the console in front of me, and the welcome ZXN37 appeared.

John placed his left hand on his outline again this time the console started to react much like the one in front of me. His screen rose from his console and displayed a schematic drawing of the craft. The drawing showed the outline of the craft, and all of the propulsion devices, the main system, and the ancillary system mounted under the outer shell of the craft. There was a green light indicating that all devices were ready to be utilized.

John moved his cursor across the screen to an icon that indicated weapons. John pressed the key down as if he were clicking a mouse. The schematic on his screen changed to show the weaponry on the leading edge of the craft, there were 144 weapon ports mounted on the leading edge of the craft. The schematic showed a separation into 16 quadrants, each quadrant showed a small green light indicating it was ready for use.

John found a menu on the right side of the screen with "Arm" "Fire" "Disarm" and "Ready" displayed on it. He moved his cursor over one of the quadrants on the schematic, and clicked on it.

The quadrant light turned red, and the "Ready" light on the menu turned on. John moved his cursor to the "Arm" indicator, and clicked on it. The "Ready" light went out, and the "Arm" light started flashing. John immediately clicked on the "Ready" indicator, and the "Armed" light went out.

We knew from that point on that we could defend the craft if the need arose. John said he thought there was a similar schematic on the smaller craft he used, but he had not looked for any defensive capabilities on the smaller craft.

We explored other schematics of the craft, the console John was to use contained all of the vital information required to defend, maintain, and operate the craft. My console had similar schematics on it, but was much more detailed about the control, and operation of the craft.

John and I were immersed in the exploration of the control consoles when a small buzzer on John's console began to sound. There was a small icon on the top left hand side of John's screen that was flashing. John clicked on the icon and a picture of the valley appeared on his screen. The picture showed the valley and a helicopter flying over the far end of it.

George and Herman came running into the cave, they ran to two separate shuttle craft, and climbed into them. The craft moved up and out of the mouth of the cave headed towards the helicopter.

The picture on John's screen showed the two shuttle craft approaching the helicopter. "The helicopter pilot will see the shuttle crafts John." I said. "Don't worry! Robert both the crafts have holographic shielding devices, the pilot of the helicopter will never know he was approached by the craft." John said.

We watched the shuttle craft approach the helicopter, and then one rose up and flew about 50 feet above the helicopter. The other shuttle craft flew a circle around the helicopter. The helicopter continued in the direction it had been travelling, there was no indication the pilot was aware of the shuttle craft were near him. Then the shuttle craft changed positions so they were in formation with the helicopter, one was on the left, and the other on the right side of the helicopter.

Suddenly the helicopter began rocking from one side to the other, and I saw the shuttle craft moving up and down rapidly. This caused a vicious series of wind gusts that was rocking the helicopter. They kept the helicopter rocking until it turned and climbed on a heading that would take it out of the valley.

"We learned to disturb the air around aircraft by accident" John said. "One day we had the 4 craft out, and were experimenting with our flying. We flew up beside an airliner. We had our holographic shields activated, and joined in formation with the airplane. Everything was fine until Steven started that rapid up and down movement. He was at the leading edge of the airplane's wing, when he moved up and down the airplane started to rock just like that helicopter. We all started the rapid up and down movement, and the airplane almost rolled over. We decided the people on the airplane deserved a better flight so we broke off the formation, and let the airplane continue on its way."

"Now if a small plane or a helicopter wanders into the valley we use the turbulence action to scare them away from the valley." That way no one will get hurt and the valley will not be explored."

We closed Venerable down, and exited the craft. I knew that I had to be present so that John, and the others could access the craft, so I was not concerned that any misuse of Venerable's capabilities would occur.

We walked over to the shuttle craft that John was able to operate, John placed his left hand on the outline, the stairs appeared, and the door on the upper level opened. We climbed the stairs, and entered the craft. John took his seat in front of the command console and I took the seat beside him. John placed his hand over the outline on the console, a soft whirring came from the craft, and the walls became translucent.

John examined the console then pointed out a small button in front of his roller ball. The button had an image that looked like a computer screen on it. He told me that he had never pressed the button, because he was to busy learning to move the craft, and control it. He pressed down on the button, and a screen rose from the console in front of him. This screen was almost identical to the one in the command centre of Venerable.

"Holy!! John exclaimed. The screen had everything that the screen in Venerable had. There was a weapon icon just like the one on Venerable, and it had the same menu. John clicked the icon and a schematic came on to the screen.

The schematic was an outline of the shuttle craft, showing all of the weapon ports imbedded in the crafts outer leading edges. There was also a bay similar to the one we found on the Venerable. The schematic also showed and on board armory with a large cache of personal weapons. It appeared as though the craft was very heavily armed.

The schematic showed that the craft's leading edge weapons were divided into 16 quadrants just as Venerable's weapons were.

There was a small green light on each quadrant, the Ready, Arm, & Fire menu was on the right hand of the screen in the same manner as we found on the Venerable.

John moved the craft ahead, and out of the cave. As we passed out of the entrance it appeared as though we had flown through a misty curtain. "The holographic shield" John said. We rose steadily over the valley until the altimeter read 450' then John brought the craft to a stop, we were hovering about a mile from a mountain that stood at the south end of the valley.

John moved his cursor to the quadrant facing the mountain, and clicked on it. The red light came indicating the quadrant was active, he clicked on the "Arm" indicator and it started flashing.

"I am going to fire the weapons, Hold on!" he said as he moved the cursor to the "Fire" indicator. He clicked on the indicator, and 3 flashes of light streaked from the craft towards the side of the mountain. In an instant the side of the mountain erupted in a huge cloud of dust.

John placed the weapons back in the "Ready" position, and then moved the craft towards the side of the mountain. When we got close to the mountain we saw a large hole that had been blown in the side. The dust was still settling, the hole appeared to be 20' in circumference, and penetrated the rock for as far as we could see in. "These are some powerful weapons; we will have to be very careful with their use." I told John. "I will shield the hole, and not tell the others how to operate the weapons." John said.

I told John it would be much better if he showed the others how to operate the weapons on the craft, than to have them discover how to do it on their own. They might experiment too, and that would not be a good thing. John agreed with my thinking, and said he would show them when he got back from my place.

John moved the craft up, and out of the valley, we climbed at an incredible rate, and were soon high above the Earth. The altimeter said 60,000 feet. There was a vapor trail on the horizon, and we headed towards it. From above it looked like a 747. John closed in on the plane from behind and we soon were travelling along above it. John kept the craft at the same speed as the plane, 500 feet above it. He explained that we could not get any closer to it because our magnetic drive disrupted the electrical system on airplanes. The craft has the same effect on vehicles, which causes them to suddenly loose power. We flew above the plane for 15 minutes, then broke off, and headed for Tofield.

We were at an altitude of 50,000 feet over Tofield when John stepped on the pedal to reduce power. Suddenly I had the sickening feeling that we were falling out of the sky, and we were. Then just as suddenly John increased the power, and the craft came to a slow rate of descent. I must have looked a little sick, because John was laughing at me.

"We can go up just as fast as we came down Robert, do you want to go back up?" John asked. "No Thanks!" I said. John went on to explain that they had learned to climb and descend early in their experiments with the craft. They then ventured to a military base; the base radar had picked them up and had scrambled a couple of jets to investigate. John and the boys let the jets get fairly close then put their craft in an accelerated climb. They were out of the jets range in a blink of an eye. When they learned how to use the holographic shielding device they had even more fun with the military pilots. The boys would turn on their shields, and watch the jets fly right on by them.

John flew the craft over Tofield, and above the open field by the monitoring station, then gently lowered it on to the open field.

I moved to the exit door, walked down the steps to the ground, turned and waved as the craft lifted off, and moved away at a very high rate of speed. In seconds it was out of sight.

I walked around to the front door of the monitoring station, and rang the bell. Johanna opened the door and let me in. We had a cup of tea, and then Johanna left. I was back in the monitoring station alone at last. I had many memories of the past 4 days, but it would take a great deal of time to understand the meaning of all I had seen.

The Final Days

The rumbling of the Earth's surface have begun earthquakes are occurring in more locations, volcanoes are erupting in lands that have been frozen for centuries. The earth scientists have measured a shift in the axis of 10cm as a result of the latest earthquakes. The earthquakes are also increasing in magnitude with one of the latest measuring 8.8 on the scale.

There is a sad phenomenon that occurs after the shock of an earthquake has subsided. Many people (Mostly Males) descend on food stores, smash their way into the store, and loot what ever is on the shelves. They carry this food off to be either consumed, or sold at very high prices to survivors of the earthquake. There is a horrible amount of wastage.

During a time of heightened tension in the world in the prior century, whenever a country was placed on high alert of an impending attack, armed guards were placed at food stores. This action was taken due to the fact there was enough food in the stores to feed the population for a period of 30 days if the food was properly rationed.

This would be the case in an earthquake area also if instead of looting the food stores the males were to guard the stores, and see to it that the food was properly rationed to the population. It will be up to those who have been awakened to the purpose of the NDE to help initiate this action.

When an earthquake occurs in a region of the world all countries rush aid to the stricken area. What would happen if there was no way this aid could reach the stricken area. If the earthquake was centered in the mid-west of the North American continent for example, with all of the airports destroyed, the bridges and roads destroyed so that no aid could reach cities, or towns in the area.

How would the populations survive if the looting scenario took place? The simple answer is the population would not survive unless some basic precautions are put in place.

There must be a conscious decision amongst the populations of earth to make plans to have armed forces, or civilian militias respond to the food stores in an area that experiences an earthquake of other natural disaster, and guard these stores against any looting. Only then would the food be rationed out to the population to ensure as many as possible were able to survive.

Sad to say there is no way that people from Sirius B, Pleiades, Orion or any other advanced civilization can make themselves known to the general population of Earth until the catastrophic events leading up to the final turn of the Earth's axis have reached a crescendo. Only then will the general population be ready to accept the presence of HEB (Highly Evolved Beings) craft coming to evacuate them from the dying planet.

There is a description of the craft that Jesus will use to make his return to Earth, found in Chapter 22, verse 16, 17, of REVELATION in the Bible. Unfortunately people who have read the description have not grasped the size of this craft. It is 12,000 furlongs, or 1500 miles and 5.28 yards wide, 1500 miles and 5.28 yards long, and of the same height. The outer wall is 144 Cubits, or 216 feet high.

One of Earth's more notable scientists has recently warned against the coming of a large ship from outer space, and alien encounters. He seeks to portray other intelligent life in the universe as a dreadful threat to human existence.

The exact opposite is true! Humans from other parts of the Universe care very deeply what happens to humans on earth, and are determined to make every effort to see that they survive.

The Human Spirit or Soul as it is known to Earth's people is Universal, and an intricate part of the ONE. In order that the ONE may experience the magnificence of the Universe it must have a body, and the Human body is that means of experiencing all that is. This is the reason that Earth Human bodies must be preserved, and nurtured.

My people are making ready for their departure at the time given by the ending of an era December 22, 2012. We will use the craft known as Venerable, which is a much smaller craft than Jesus's "Jerusalem".

I have written this manuscript in an effort to alert the people of Earth's minds to the possibility that a greater experience will come to them in the near future. There is still time to accept the WAY, and begin to live with the new Commandment given by Jesus. "That ye love one another; as I have loved you, that ye also love one another." This is all inclusive regardless of Race, Color, or Creed.

Every living human on the face of the Earth has the opportunity of being evacuated by "Jerusalem" the only requirement to be met is the Free Will acceptance of the WAY.

Be as ONE

Zxn37

"Those of the Way do not enforce truth upon one another,
We help each other find it."